From Gigolo to Jesus

A Journey From Misogyny to Monogamy

By

K.L. Belvin

Bravin Publishing LLC

Published by

Bravin Publishing, LLC
P.O. Box 340317
Jamaica, New York

Copyright © 2011 K.L. Belvin

All rights reserved, including the right of reproduction in whole or part in any form. No part of this book may be used or reproduced in any manner, whatsoever, without permission except in the case of brief quotations embodied in critical articles and reviews.

ISBN-13: 978-0-9845018-1-6
ISBN-10: 0-9845018-1-9

Cover by G8 Visual Designs

Interior Designed by Bravin Publishing, LLC
www.bravinpublishing.com

Library of Congress Control Number 2010918028

Printed in the United States of America

"Wow is all I can say. Great book. Didn't put it down once. It touched me."

– D. Diamond

"Started reading and the book is deep. I was so into it I missed my stop on the train. Can't wait to finish it."

–S. Lee

"I read it in one day. I am very pleased with the outcome. If lives aren't transformed from this book, then there is no hope. Your openness was amazing. God has truly blessed you with Tiffany and her love for you Keith."

-J. Ottley

"Everyone can come away from this book having learned something to either take to heart, or help someone they know with the information provided in this book. It's a powerful testimony that millions will benefit from."

-T. Hardin

"This book is a reality check for all individuals who have or are currently damaging their lives and the lives of others."

– Jay Smith, Playwright and Author of "Piece of Me"

Contents

Acknowledgements 1
Foreword 3
Introduction 4
Teenage Years 6
Sex vs Love 18
The Addiction 29
Abortions & Miscarriages 33
Being Married (The First Time) 40
Big Beautiful Women & The Internet 57
Becoming a Father 63
The Motel 72
Hearing The Lord's Voice & Finding Love 80
Bible Study 104
Paying For Your Sins 109
My Growing Family 118
Becoming a Writer 139
Conclusion 145

Acknowledgements

First and foremost I want to thank the Lord for not giving up on reaching out to me and saving my life. I want to thank my lovely wife, Tiffany, on helping me get this book completed. I know it took a minute to complete, but we did it. Who knew when we laid eyes on each other in college we would someday be in position to help others reach their dreams. I am truly a better man with you in my life. I couldn't see myself living with and for anyone else. You are my blessing from the Lord.

To my grandmother, thank you for reminding me, over all these years, I was destined to be a man of God. Thank you for your never-ending prayers for all of us in this family and for always being there when I needed someone to talk to. I love you with all of my heart.

To my family, we have had our differences, but I pray the Lord grants you all peace and blessings. Love always.

To my children, Jonathan, Kierra, Anthony, Elijah, and Justin I love you all and pray all of you find the success the Lord has tucked away deep inside you.

To my Christian Brother and fellow Educator, Michael Bostic, all the days we spent trying to teach today's children you never let me forget you were a child of God. It was your knowledge of the Word which led me to call on you when I heard the calling from the Lord. My time spent in bible study changed my life forever.

Thine Johnson, John Harris, Curt Richardson—my dudes, thank you for support over the years. Thank you for remaining cool with me after I found the Lord. I know we don't hit the streets anymore, but I am glad you're still a part of my life.

To my friend and ex-girlfriend, Jacqueline Ottley, years ago you saw in me what the Lord created, even when I couldn't see it or understand it. Your friendship and the fact you have remained exactly who you claimed to be shows what a blessing you are.

How could I ever forget all the fun we had and all the spades we played? Mr. and Mrs. Hall did a wonderful job with you and your family.

To all of my readers, thank you for taking the time to consider this book. This is a testimony I pray helps someone who is trying to find themselves just as I was. Please don't hesitate to share what you have learned with anyone you think needs help.

God Bless you all.

K. L. Belvin,
Former Gigolo turned Loving husband.

Foreword

I can recall KL, or Big Dog, as I affectionately call him, coming home and telling me that one of his friends was not happy with "the new" KL. The friend reminisced about all of the fun they had and how much time they spent together running amuck. He told him that he wished that he had the old KL back. I listened to Big Dog's saddened tone as he spoke about his friend of many years and when he was finished I asked him how he felt about the new KL. He responded, "I'm happy and unfortunately he just doesn't get it."

That evening when I went to bed I prayed for my husband, as I do every night. However, I cried as I prayed. I cried because I know that Big Dog's friend meant well, but he couldn't fathom what he was asking for. For five years I had a front row seat to the self-destructive path that Big Dog called his life. In the public eye he was big man on campus, the life of the party, the one everybody thought had it all together, but in private he was falling apart.

I am in constant gratitude to our Holy Father that he has delivered Big Dog from that place. Every day added to his transition is like a day of sobriety that we celebrate together.

Tiffany Braxton Belvin,
Wife of a former gigolo.

Introduction

Watch out for those dogs. Those men who do evil. Those manipulators of the flesh. Ephesians 3:2.

In The Bible, God warned against men, like me, who are liars, cheaters, destroyers of dreams and who treacherously feed their ravenous sexual desires. I am not proud to admit that I was among those predators for more than three decades of my life, but I can honestly say that I am proof that change is possible. My transformation was not an easy one and the greatest battle was admitting that I was as venomous as they come.

While I didn't physically beat or rape women nor did I force myself on anyone. I learned, like a lion on the prowl, how to hide in the tall grass, watch my victims, and understand their weaknesses. I hunted my prey and that prey was women. I was extremely effective at acquiring the hearts of my victims who honestly believed I cared. In reality my goal was to feed my addiction by manipulating someone else's emotions because I felt I had lost my own soul.

When people hear the term gigolo they automatically think of a man who receives money from women for his sexual services. As I enhanced my craft of enticing women I was compensated with gifts, trips, and expensive restaurants, among other things. You see, a gigolo has to be a great liar. He has to be a chameleon so that he becomes whatever you need him to be. That is his appeal. I would love to say, sexually, I was the best man on the planet, but my gift as well as my curse is I understand how women think. I also understand how sex could manipulate women and I made it work for me.

So, I believed that I was happy. I had fixed a facade around myself to such a degree that I had other people believing I was happy, and hoping that if I told enough lies I would find the happiness that I didn't have. This book is going to take you on a journey of where that unhappiness began. I was a young man so out of control that I believed the only thing that could save my life was jail or death. I knew I didn't want to end up in jail so I figured out how to do things to stay clear of it. However, I certainly didn't want death.

From Gigolo to Jesus focuses on men as predators based on my own experiences and observations. Keep in mind I have observed men and women play both roles as victim and villain. Hopefully, in reading, you will identify which one you are and be encouraged to make some changes. Consider where you are in your life and if you're happy.

Teenage Years

Ephesians 6:4 – New American Standard Bible. Fathers do not provoke your children to anger but bring them up in the discipline and instruction of the Lord.

Mothers do a tremendous job in raising young men in the best way they know how. Lord knows my mother and grandmother tried to instill values that would make me a better person. They preached, they lectured, they even threatened, but what they could not be is my father. When a male authority is absent from the home the vital bonding and nurturing between a boy and his father is also absent. I needed that male authority and the unique bond formed by father and son. I did not have it and the consequences were severe.

At an early age, I learned of two betrayals. The father I knew abandoned me, but in fact, my biological father had abandoned me *before* I was born. I once heard a minister on the radio say, "To complete a puzzle a person will look on the box because the picture will become their guide, and so as they put the puzzle together they use it to steer them in the direction they need to go to make sure they get the finished product." Think of a father being that picture or that guide. When it is torn away or smudged then the fatherless child is left to his own accord and to piece the puzzle together on his own.

What my mother and grandmother also didn't realize is my environment had already begun shaping what would become my character and nothing they said changed it. My mother was seventeen years old when she had me and my grandmother was fifteen years old when she had her; both raised children without the respective fathers. Growing up I watched the men they dated and none of them were candidates for being the role model I needed.

My mom and grandmother, both, were often victims of abusive and sometimes violent relationships with men. This fueled my disdain and hatred towards male authority figures. My wife also believes it fueled my dislike and disrespect for women. I internalized my rage and it aided me in becoming a predatory monster. So, the question is how did I learn to become a man? It was a long and ongoing process so let's start at the beginning.

I moved from a small town in southern New Jersey to New York City when I was about ten years old. It was stimulation overload. It was like I traveled to a different planet with so many people, things moving so fast, and everything seemed to be so readily available. It was too easy to go down the wrong path. By the age of twelve I started to discover my body, what certain parts were capable of, and how it made me feel especially towards the opposite sex. I started looking past the comic books in the local bodegas trying to steal a peak at the naked bodies on the porn magazines. Back then dirty magazines were our internet and cable television fix. So, eventually, my curiosities got the best of me and lead to me stealing my first magazine—stuck it right in between the Sunday newspaper and walked out the door. It wouldn't be the last magazine I stole.

Jackpot! I became addicted to pornography. It was like I had heroin mainlined, snorted cocaine, smoked marijuana, or had my first drink of alcohol. I became so addicted I couldn't think of anything else. I wanted to learn as much as I could about sex. I'd give my allowance to the older guys to buy magazines when I didn't steal them. Being raised by my mother and grandmother, I had two women in the house so I had to learn how to keep things hidden because my mother and grandmother were in and about my room on a regular. I had to learn how to hide things in shoe boxes and baseball equipment. Anywhere I could keep the dirty magazines so they couldn't get to them. I would hide things deep in the "throw-away" closet that many African-American families have.

These magazines were my first lessons in sex and I absorbed them like a sponge. I didn't just look at the pictures, I read the articles. I'd read them back and forth sometimes more than once to get my fix. I was in training mode. However, like any training of a skill, there comes the time when you have to put it to action. I was ready, but I couldn't see I was slowly destroying my childhood.

It wasn't hard finding my first victim. "Magdaline" may not have thought she was a victim, and instead a willing participant, but, like me, she too was a victim of her circumstance. She was a member of a family that was known for their promiscuity, including the mother. She had not even become a teenager yet, but already had multiple sexual partners and was smart enough to know what to do and not do during sex.

I used to convince Magdaline to come with me to a little hideaway in one of the buildings of our complex. Each building had an incinerator for trash in the basement and often the maintenance workers would forget to lock the doors at night. That's where people went to hang out, get high, or take a girl that was ready to give it up. It was filthy, gritty, and smelled, but when you're a sexually charged twelve-year-old it can seem like a palace. She and I would "play doctor". I'd touch parts on her body and she'd touch parts on mine. I liked the reaction I got from her and she liked the reaction she got from me. All that playing and touching eventually led to her coming to my house.

I remember the day so clearly. Everyone was outside because it was a warm summer day. There was no reason to be in the house, but I had an agenda. My mother and grandmother worked full-time so that gave enough opportunity for us to be in the house alone. I convinced Magdaline to come to the apartment. I finally had the opportunity to act out all of the things I had been reading and dreaming about through hours of masturbation. Armed with the knowledge from the pornographic magazines and a willing partner, she let me take her clothes off. She let me do to her what I read in the magazines. I didn't know if I was doing it right. I didn't use protection or even know I was supposed to. All I knew was it felt really good. I was becoming a man, performing manly acts, but still with a child's mind.

After lying down with this young lady for what seemed like three hours, but was in fact about three minutes, I had my first ejaculation through intercourse. It was paralyzing. Like a lightning bolt had gone through my whole body. This was the making of a sexual junkie. As I lay on the bed dazed she asked me had I ejaculated inside of her. How did this twelve-year-old know that I was supposed to take it out before the explosion? The magazines didn't talk about taking it out. I never understood what those big words meant anyway so I kind of skipped over them. When I couldn't give her a definitive answer she got dressed very quickly and ran off. Because I had never been taught, I didn't even know I was supposed to walk her to the door.

I remember sleeping for a couple of hours and finally waking up with a new set of eyes. I had come out of the shell of my twelve-year-old body and now moved into what was going to be my future. My mind was no longer focused on little league baseball and football it was now filled with how I could get the next little girl into my bed and how I could get Magdaline back into the house to let me do it to her again. The little boy inside me died, and in its place was the birth of this unguided soul. In hindsight, I realize I had just laid the track for what the next thirty years of my life would become.

For the next couple of years my appetite grew as well as my ability to convince women to let me do what I wanted to them. Often, we watch movies which give men credit for having "game". We also have music videos that promote pimping which is simply a man's ability to convince a woman to have sex with other men for money and bring the money back to him. The pimp uses lies, sexual prowess, and sometimes physical violence as a way to convince her that he is the most important entity in her life. Hence, the prostitute calls the pimp Daddy. I had become somewhat of a teenage pimp. I didn't make women go out and sleep with other men, but I convinced young ladies to have sex with me. I don't know if you can be a thirteen-year-old sex addict, but I think I was as close as I could come. I mean there were times that I could go without it, but you know what? Now that I think about it, I may have been an addict. I wanted sex and would have sex with anyone that would let me.

To parents reading this book right now I want you to understand what I am about to say. When you see your son participating in unhealthy behaviors that are detrimental to a relationship do not say it is just a part of a boy growing up. It does not have to be the case. Though I tried to hide my indiscretions from my mom and grandmother as best I could, they saw the revolving door of girls. They allowed it because they thought it was the best way for me to learn to become a man. This was definitely ironic because they were allowing me to become just like the men I watched victimize them throughout the years. What they should have been trying to get through to me is respect for women. It starts with a healthy understanding of what a real relationship is; sharing of affection and compassion for the other person. Do not allow your son to view women as collateral property for their manhood.

Most of my understanding of how to be with women came from my friends and the older guys in the street. Many of them came from homes like mine with single mothers or fathers who didn't spend enough time with them. So, I learned women were like trophies. You carry them around for a little while, put them on display so you can boast about your "win" then when they got dusty and tarnished and you grew tired of looking at them you threw them in the closet. On occasion you bring them out again just to look at them and reminisce on your glory days.

Keep in mind, also, the more virtuous the more valuable to my collection. A young lady's virginity meant nothing to me, but another obstacle to overcome and another "prize" to my collection. It proved how tight my game was if she let down her guard to allow me to become her first. So, of course I had to be more convincing, more beguiling, and a little more patient. I learned from the book of street knowledge when you have a virgin be very easy and take your time because this is her first time. She's scared and it may cause her some pain, and you don't want to hurt her, at first. Give her time to get comfortable with you. Once she's comfortable, then you give it to her like you just got home from jail. Give it to her hard and fast. She may cry a little bit. She may ask you to stop. Ignore her. Make her remember you because you're her first. If she bleeds, that's even better. Just remember to pull out so you don't get her pregnant, but up until that point, try to hurt her as much as you can because she'll remember you and if you're her first, you'll always have a way back in.

This was not making love because love had nothing to do with it; it was about conquering and this was how I had sex. As sick as it sounds this is a standard practice in urban neighborhoods. Older abused boys trying to teach younger abused boys. No monogamy. No morals. No God. There was nothing to let me know that it's not how you treat a woman. Armed with foolishness I acted like a fool. With the pornography as my bible, and with other followers of the pornography way, this is how I set out to make a name for me and it got worse.

By the time I was sixteen years old my home structure had changed significantly. My mother, sister, and aunt moved out of the two bedroom apartment we shared with my grandmother and her boyfriend. I convinced my mom to let me continue living with my grandmother. This gave me an opportunity to have the apartment to myself for a decent part of the day because my grandmother worked from three in the afternoon until eleven in the evening. Her boyfriend also worked at night. For a seven to nine hour period I was left alone. It's said idle minds are the devil's playground. My grandmother's place became my playground. Getting girls to sleep with me had become routine. They were making it too easy for me and my ego. I ran through as many women in my immediate apartment complex as I could. Then when I got bored I travelled to one of my friend's neighborhood who lived about twenty minutes away. It gave me the variety I needed to keep me entertained for as long as it could.

There was a different turn of events when one day my aunt forgot her keys and asked me to bring them to her job. As I walked into the office one of my aunt's coworkers, Cathy asked "Who is this handsome young man?" My aunt introduced us. Cathy continued to comment on how handsome I was. Now this cougar could have just been being polite, but my mind was in pimp mode and I had a new target. I'm a big game hunter and this older woman was much bigger game than the gazelles that I had been chasing. How do I get something I've never had before: a grown woman? After we finished taking visual inventory of each other we shook hands. Cathy smiled and asked if I played sports. I told her I did. She asked how old I was. I told her I was sixteen years old. Then she told me I looked much older and made a comment on the amount of facial hair I had. I smiled eating up all the compliments and thought to myself, "She's going to make this easy."

Shortly after getting home my phone rang. It was Cathy.

"What are you doing?" She asked me.

"Laying on the couch", I responded.

"Do you know why I called you?

Now, any parent of a young teen boy knows at this point there should be a red flag going up in the air and this conversation shouldn't be taking place. Cathy was over forty-years-old and had no, explicable, reason for calling me.

"No, I don't."

"Well, I live in the Bronx. My aunt lives out there where you live and I'm coming out there. I thought you would like to get together and go get something to eat."

My ears and my loins sprang to attention. I went straight into pimp mode. Keep in mind I had no tactful way of doing it either.

"Why do we have to go get lunch?" I asked her. "Why don't you just come here?"

"Come to your house?"

"Yes, come to my house."

Later, I learned Cathy had four children including a son older than me, but it didn't matter to her and it definitely didn't matter to me. However, this desperate and lustful woman victimized and used me. I know some of you are reading this now saying she made me a man, but if this was a sixteen-year-old girl with a forty-something-year-old man would you feel the same way? Yes, there is a double standard between the genders. However, Cathy was on the verge of arming me with knowledge I had no business having. Worse, she was further cultivating my disrespect for women. She lowered herself to my level. In my mind I was already a sexual king among my peers and thought I was greater than what I actually was. Cathy had now made me her Daddy because I was pimping her.

"Well, is anyone going to be there?" She asked the question that any worried parent would ask, but of course Daddy has an answer.

"Of course not, why would Daddy ask you to come over?"

How many sixteen-year-olds do you know can get a grown woman to take a day off from work so he can have his way with her? She got to my house about three-thirty in the afternoon. She was dressed conservatively, but it didn't matter what she had on because it was all about to come off anyway.

Like any woman she wanted to talk. Break the ice and warm up to intimacy, but I didn't understand small talk and I didn't know what foreplay was. All I knew is how to grab, prod, and have sex. So that's exactly what I did. In the midst of doing what I do, she stopped me.

"What are you doing?" She seemed annoyed.

"I'm trying to have sex with you."

"Not like that," she barked.

"Not like what? This is what I do," I answered as smooth and confidently as I could.

She looked at me with nurturing eyes, but not as a mother to a child. She was going to mold me and teach me how to satisfy her sexually. She was going to show me how a man is supposed to make love to a woman. In one instant Cathy raped me of my childhood. No she didn't physically hurt me. She didn't force me to have sex with her. Instead, she armed me with knowledge that I should not have had in a body I could not control which had the mental focus of an untamed animal. She had now set the wild animal loose.

You can't put a young man in a situation where acting like an animal is going to benefit him because once you do that young man has the ability to evolve into something awful. So now here's another transformation. What I have morphed into was worse than the last. Because Cathy was showing me how a woman's body can react to me I started to learn another level of my craft. I'm being tested and I'm passing the tests with flying colors because of stamina and my eagerness to learn.

Cathy and I stopped seeing each other at my house because she wanted to see me more often. One day she invited me to the Bronx and we walked around the zoo. Others would have normally viewed us as mother-son spending time together. However, it was actually an older woman talking to the younger man with the idea of showing him how he can become a much better predator. That was the illusion. What you actually had was a date. While we were there I pretended to enjoy being at the zoo, but I was more excited about what would happen afterwards.

We went into an apartment building right across the street. In a dingy staircase smelling of urine Cathy got on her knees and gave me my first experience of oral pleasure. Even when one of the male tenants came down the steps and saw us, you would think that would have been enough to make us leave from embarrassment. Instead, the man congratulated me and like a well paid prostitute Cathy looked up and smiled. As the gentlemen walked by he said, "Show Shorty what he needs to know," giving his seal of approval.

For the next five to six months we met each other four to five times a week. She would pay for the hotel rooms and then afterwards stick twenty to forty dollars in my pocket. I was Daddy now.

The additional damage is she now set this wild animal loose on young women who weren't prepared to defend themselves against someone like me. That's another danger of an older woman exploiting a younger man. Now, when I would meet younger women, my game was smoother and refined. I would walk up to any women and be flirtatious knowing that if I could use it to get anywhere close to a bed, I could show them the techniques I was taught. I could perform several times a day and my recovery was that of just pure fury. Yet my psyche was still that of a pubescent boy. I was still making my rounds with the young ladies in my neighborhood. With my new bravado I was showing them the skills I learned. At the same time, Cathy started to bore me and things began to wind down.

Before it did, however, towards the end of our relationship Cathy invited a girlfriend to join in our sexual escapades. One day I took the long ride on the bus from Queens to the Bronx. When I got to the hotel I was annoyed to see her standing there with someone else because I was thinking we were going to do what we do. Now, this was going to throw a wrench in it. Cathy introduced me to Faye. She was about the same age as Cathy and I could see the eagerness in her face. Cathy told Faye all about her boy toy and was now willing to share me. We all went into the hotel room.

"Do you think you can do to Faye the things you do to me?" Cathy opened up the door to something I had not even imagined.

At that point bells started to ring, in my mind, like I just hit the jackpot in Las Vegas. The man in the designer suit just handed me the big check.

"Of course, I can do to Faye what I do to you," I responded, "Are you okay with that?"

It really didn't matter to me if she wasn't, but when you are a pimp you always want to make the woman feel as if she is doing what she wants to do not because you want her to.

"Sure."

About a month later I was caught in my game. My mother had been curious about who I was spending all this time with. I admitted how old Cathy was and my mother gave her a call.

"Listen here, b----, this is a *boy* that you're laying with and if you're so uncomfortable with yourself that you gotta lay with little boys, you need to find something else to do with yourself. I better never catch you around my son or calling the house ever again."

It was a weak threat, at best, because my mother didn't live with me and my grandmother was working. No one could stop me if I really wanted to continue the relationship, but like I said I started getting bored. I absorbed all I could from her and I definitely didn't want my mother coming around so I had an easy out. Cathy didn't give up though. She called quite a few times after, but I always used the excuse that I didn't want to get in trouble with my mother. How ridiculous that must have sound that a forty-year-old woman is begging to see a boy that still needs to get permissions from his mother.

I continued to slowly destroy myself. It was like a rock being transformed by running water. You don't see the changes right away, but give it time and you realize that the rock you see today wasn't the same a few hundred years ago. I began to excel in my social life, but school was definitely beginning to suffer because I found something that kept my attention even more than sports. I went from being a very gifted student to a barely above average student. My teen years, what should have normally been the happiest times for any kid, were the worst for me. I was kicked out of my high school and forced to go to an alternative school for wayward kids. Eventually, my grandmother felt the best thing for me to do was leave New York altogether and she sent me back to New Jersey.

My grandmother is the matriarch of my immediate family and most decisions are not made without her input. If I knew then, what I know now, I probably would have shared much of what I was going through with her so she could understand why I had transformed into this monster.

Most teenagers won't tell their parents what they are dealing with. They'll share it with their friends or they'll keep it locked away. It's worse for teenagers without fathers directly in their lives. Those teens transform into the anger that the Lord speaks about in the bible. Their anger will fuel decisions that will affect the rest of their lives. Often, in ways they will never be able to recover and those absentee fathers are the direct fault of that. So, I ask that fathers open the door to their children. The older they become before you do the harder it will be to mend those fences. Between the ages of thirteen to twenty-one they'll be afraid to let you in especially if you were not there regularly from the beginning.

As parents we can't allow anyone to slide past our defenses. Don't allow anyone to get close enough to your son or daughter until you have armed them with the positives and negatives of their actions in relationships. Arm them with more self worth than they can hold. Help them to understand that they are the anchor to their soul; that God will be there to protect them even if they have to stand all by themselves. Use *every* ounce of the nurturing powers that God has given you. Form a hedge around your children such that you are there even when they don't see you.

I don't advocate staying in a relationship just because you have children, but I do implore mothers and fathers to think twice about any decisions they make regarding their relationship when children are involved. For those parents who are still together the unity that you bring to the table is a bond that your children can use in defense against this nasty world that we live in. Bring them in and allow that energy that you two have for each other to engulf your children. Make your children as much a part of that unity as anything else because as you already know, what's out there does not promote unity, it promotes death. When God is absent, the only thing left is death.

Sex vs Love

I didn't know what love was supposed to be between partners. The only love I had experienced was from my family, and because there was no male role model to show me how a man is supposed to act towards his mate I was oblivious to the fact that there should be love in my relationships and in fact I should have chosen my relationships better. One of the things that a young man will come across in his life, once he gives into his sexual nature, is he will now have to deal with the emotions that come with sexual feelings. As a man when you have chosen to connect sexually with different women then you have to deal with the different emotions that come with them.

The only preference I had when it came to women was you had to be full-figured. If you were smaller than a size fourteen I wasn't looking at you, but other than that your appearance, education, financial status, career, neither physical nor mental impairments were obstacles for me. I didn't care how many children you had, if you had just come out of a messed up relationship, or if you were currently in one. I didn't even have to be physically attracted to you, in all honesty. Full-figured women who are thought to be less attractive were easier manipulating because they weren't used to receiving attention.

I need to interject here that in addition to plus-sized women, I also have affection for ghetto girls. The "ghetto girl" refers to women that come from low economic situations, and tend not to stray far from it. The saying is "You can take the girl out of the ghetto, but you can't take the ghetto out of the girl." When dealing with a ghetto girl, often, you'll deal with women that have lower expectations and aspirations for themselves. They become easier targets for sexual escapades because their self-esteem or self-worth may be limited or jaded. Once you understand how to pay them the attention needed, make them feel comfortable, then the opportunity to have sex is there. There are ghetto girls that feel, and in some cases, have been taught by the ghetto women that have raised them that it's their duty to have sex with you simply because you took them on a date or treated them nice. It's their way of showing their appreciation.

Prostitute, ghetto girl, or business woman none of it mattered if you were not a plus-sized woman. Now, to clarify, I didn't target plus-sized women. My aesthetic preference is a plus-sized woman. However, I have to admit women of size are easy targets because they are constantly under attack by society. All I had to do is become something a little bit different than the norm and the doors were open. You could spot the insecurities right away. Giving well placed comments or taking note of something minute as the color of her nail polish could go further than you would believe. All of the things that women think matters didn't then and doesn't matter to men who are only looking to have sex because once your clothes come off you are no different than that last chick they bedded.

On the inside, however, I wanted to have a girlfriend who I could care about, but didn't understand why I even wanted it. I had a desire to be loved; not knowing it was love, while sex was clearly at the steering wheel. I always had someone I called my girlfriend while still trying to sleep with everyone else. When I was 18 years old I had a girlfriend that I met through a friend. She was the first woman I actually felt love for. Everything about her fascinated me. The way she spoke, walked, and smelled captivated me. It was something I'd never experienced before and even then I knew it was love. When we first met we must have talked for about four hours then exchanged numbers. Later on that day we talked for another couple of hours. So, I knew this was different because all of my previous relationships began and ended with "When are we going to have sex?"

"Jill" and I began dating and instead of me listening to my parents advice that I needed to be with one woman I honestly believed there was nothing wrong with me having a girlfriend that I loved and treated well, but at the same time having other women that I used on occasion to have sex with. I didn't know that you weren't supposed to have other women when you had someone you were calling your "girlfriend." In my world as long as I could keep the whorish man that I was separated from the man that I was trying to be with this young lady then the world was good. I didn't apply any pressure to her to have sex: one, because I actually respected her and two, because I had other women to take care of me if I needed. I learned to be romantic and nurturing. The loving young man that my mother was trying to raise was slowly coming forth.

Jill and I had the typical boyfriend-girlfriend scenario. She came to my basketball games to cheer me on. She wore my school jacket. When I think back God had blessed me with an equal because *all* of my weaknesses were her strengths. My callousness and ego were tempered by her humility and passion for life. She was a great singer and I loved to listen to her. Where her self-esteem was shaken, I had extra and I refused to allow anyone to speak negatively of her.

She took up more of my mind and time than I was used to any one woman having, but like Dr. Jekyll and Mr. Hyde once I had hung up the phone, took her home, and she was no longer around I became that other side of me. I evolved into a creature with two faces and those faces switched back and forth when needed. This creature operated unabated for some time, but you can't live in New York City with a population of five to seven million people and not run into someone who knows you, knows of you, and or knows the current person you're dating. My ego allowed me to think I was greater than that.

As our relationship grew and we started to come upon the holidays Jill and I had agreed we were going to keep gift giving very simple. This was one of the greatest experiences, outside of sex, that I had ever had in a relationship. It was honestly the first. Jill gave me a stuffed toy Garfield cat because she knew I was a fan of the cartoon. When it was my turn to give a gift I decided to do it at school. Anyone who knows me knows that even when I do something *simple* it has to be grandiose. We were sitting in the main lounge where all the students hung out waiting for their next class. On one side was a wall of windows from floor to ceiling. I could see when a friend of mine came out of her car with the gift I was giving Jill. It was a huge stuffed toy horse. I stepped outside and when I came back I was carrying this gigantic horse on my back. I crave attention so it was nothing for me to stand on a table in the middle of the lounge and explain to everyone that the stuffed animal was for my lovely girlfriend. I almost fell off the table, but everyone laughed.

A few hours later I overheard her tell a girlfriend she wanted a Fendi pocketbook. I had no idea who or what Fendi was, but I could hear the excitement in her voice about having one. I was big on romantic statements and I was going to try to do something special. Armed with grant money that was supposed to be for my tuition, I decided to get a Fendi bag for her for Christmas. I was told the place to get it was Macy's department store. The Christmas Holiday in New York is not just happy greetings and good cheer. You have overcrowded streets, cranky pedestrians, and tempers pushed to the limits at times. It was bedlam, but I was determined to get a gift to impress my girlfriend.

When I walked into Macy's I was immediately in a sea of bodies scurrying back and forth. It was like every movie you have seen of New York City, but multiply it by ten. Between the Christmas music, the noise, and the voices it was easy to become overwhelmed, but I was powered by love. I was so focused that it was almost silent as I looked for a salesperson to help me find Fendi. Instead I found a neat and professionally dressed security guard standing to the side.

"Good evening, where can I find a Fendi bag?" I asked him. He points to a whole section that is screaming Fendi and says, "Right over there, stupid." Wow, only in New York can a young man ask about a very expensive designer and be called stupid at the same time.

As I walked over to the Fendi section, a very friendly looking saleswoman was smiling at me. She was about in her late to mid thirties and I could tell that she'd been working at the store for a long time because as soon as I asked her about purchasing a bag for my girlfriend her eyes immediately lit up and she went straight into her sales pitch. Pulling out each bag placing them on the counter explaining what they're used for and their different features. I started to become overwhelmed. Now, I can hear the noise of all the people around me. The holiday music is starting to sound deafening. I'm feeling pressure because I don't know which bag to choose. So, like the ghetto kid that I was I based my decision on how much money I had in my pocket

"Which of these bags can I get for two-hundred dollars?"

You would have thought that I had just spit the "B" word at her. The saleswomen turned pale. Her smile disappeared and she looked as if she had been disrespected. She snatched all of the bags off the counter and starts to put what looked like miniature versions of the same bags onto the counter. They didn't come with any speech. They didn't come with any elaborate sales technique like she had just done for those other bags. It was, "Here you go."

There were basically three bags. One looked like a mutant tootsie roll with a little tiny change purse. Another one looked like a gigantic cigarette case, and the last one looked like a long wallet. She's gives me the prices of the tootsie roll and the bag with no handle which I found out later was a clutch. Now, of course, when you're young and in love, none of that matters. It's Fendi and it was *real* Fendi. Even though I didn't know I could have gone out on the street and saw one of the street vendors who could have given me the knock-off version for maybe twenty-five dollars, but when you're in love, you do stupid things. This was my stupid thing. So, I went with the clutch. It was two-hundred forty dollars, but because the saleswoman just wanted to make the sale she gave it to me for $200. I headed back to Jamaica, Queens with a smile on my face.

Jill was due to come to my house Christmas morning because we agreed I would go with her to her grandmother's house Christmas night. She had Christmas breakfast with my mother, sisters and me. After we all settled down and got comfortable in the living room I gave Jill her gift. We had already exchanged gifts so she wasn't expecting anything else.

"What is this?"

This is where, when I look back at myself, I realize that the man I am now had roots in me then. The seeds were there, but the weeds of the sexual beast and creature that I was were so in control of my life that those seeds had to take refuge in the mud which was my soul only to come out when they knew they were safe. Watching her tear open the wrapping paper was similar to watching a holiday movie and the characters are right at that moment when they are going to get their wish from Santa Claus.

She opened the box with the clutch inside. She picked the clutch up never taking her eyes off of it. I could see tears began to form in her eyes as her fingers slowly caressed it. There was complete silence as the tears now started to roll down her cheeks. When she looked up at me with those eyes, it didn't matter what I went through to get the bag. I had accomplished what I wanted and that was to send from my heart to her heart how I felt. Oh, I can still feel the hug and I can still feel the kiss and I can still feel that excitement of that moment.

Christmas evening I met Jill's family. The family wasn't too impressed with me. It was as if they could see past my charm into my devious heart. Jill's mother had a soft spot for me, though, because she could tell that I was troubled, but she could also see that there were values given to me. I had the potential to be a better person.

I remember being angry that night. Jill's family ignored me the entire time. They laughed together, reminisced together, but no one spoke to me. I felt as left out at this Christmas party as a person could ever feel. It didn't make a difference what I tried to do I stood out. So, I found myself a nice comfortable spot and I sat by myself. Jill came and found me and kept me company. She made me a plate of food and didn't leave my side until the family asked her to sing.

Jill could sing. Her voice was as if God was standing right next to her holding her hand, nodding approval. It's like the humming of the birds and they are in perfect harmony. That was her gift. When she opened her mouth and sang you *had* to listen. You know when someone's a good singer, when you close your eyes because you want to hear *all* of the words. I stood at the top of the stairs angry instead of enjoying Jill's singing like everyone else. Instead of enjoying that moment for what it was, I was thinking about me. That's the evilness that was inside of me. At a moment when I should have allowed myself to be taken in by such a blessed time and enjoy and become one, I had become one all to myself. I started thinking I wasn't supposed to be there. Not because I didn't love my girlfriend, but because I was sitting there angry about why no one paid any attention to me.

A couple of days after the dinner the matriarch of their family took ill. I remember taking Jill to the hospital a couple of different times to be there in support of her, but actually angry that I had to be there because I didn't like being around her family. Once, she even asked me to go into the room where her grandmother was. I remember going into the room with her to stand around the bed and I felt very uncomfortable because I knew no one wanted me there. Still, I was trying to support my girlfriend.

The last time we were at the hospital, before Jill's grandmother passed, I came out of the hospital room with her. She was very emotional and I was trying to support her. A male family member stood up and asked, "Why are you here? No one knows you! You didn't know my grandmother. Why are you here? You need to go."

Instead of understanding that it was just his pain causing him to react that way, I lashed back as the young, defiant, negative and nasty young man that I was, "Who are you to tell me what to do? I'm not here for you. I'm here for her so you need to mind your business." So here I am, ready to start a fight in the hospital for a grandmother that's not mine simply because *I* was disrespected. Never once thinking I needed to close my mouth and simply walk away with my girlfriend and comfort her. Going forward, I used that moment as an excuse to not be around.

When Jill's grandmother passed it was so sudden that the family had no time to plan. They needed to take care of so much paperwork in a short amount of time. Jill left school that semester because she was dealing with the situation of her grandmother. Each time I called the house her family wouldn't put through my calls because they said they needed to keep the phone lines open because they had family coming in from all over the country. I had no idea the family was so large. I didn't know the grandmother's death created so much disruption in the family and so many details had to be worked out. Today, I understand what goes into having to oversee the arrangements after someone has died, but then I didn't understand anything that didn't have me at the forefront. I surely didn't understand why my girlfriend couldn't make time for me even though her grandmother passed away. I started to mope around in school. It was all over my face that something was wrong. It was just a matter of time before someone would acknowledge and soothe my bruised ego. That person was Kimberly.

Often, a young man like me would have a girlfriend in the neighborhood, another girlfriend at school, and then possibly another one he worked with. However, Kimberly went to school with us and she also lived in our neighborhood. She had tried for a long time to get close to me, but because I didn't want to get caught cheating I didn't bother with her. I figured she was just too close to the inner circle and I didn't want that drama. Things changed when Jill became preoccupied with her grandmother's death and the needs of her family.

Kimberly also fed right into what I wanted. She told me what I wanted to hear, "Listen, I understand Jill's grandmother died, but I don't understand why she can't make time for you." She should have told me that I was stupid and selfish for being upset that Jill had to tend to her family's needs, but perhaps she was as selfish as I was.

She used my pain to get in. We have seen it in many women. They use normal circumstances in relationships to point out faults in your wife or girlfriend in order to secure their position with you. "Oh, she doesn't do this for you?" "I would never do that if I was your girlfriend." Once Kimberly got close and she found a way to spend more time with me my need and want for sex started to override my feelings for Jill. Not realizing if I had stood my ground with Kimberly and told her that I didn't want what she was offering it would have saved me a lot of misfortune. I should have been mature enough to tell her I'm going to hold myself together until my girlfriend can work out her situation with her family and when she does, I'll be the man that she needs me to be. Instead, I took all of my selfish frustration and wrapped it into one afternoon of meaningless sexual entertainment. The evil that was me took the wheel and said, "Well, fine! Let's find a replacement. We have one. Let's play with her for awhile until your girl comes back." Kimberly couldn't wait to tell her friends. Like a virus it was all over school that we had been together. Never did I stop to think that it would get back to Jill.

By Valentine's Day I had already decided that because Jill wouldn't be there I would go with Kimberly to the school dance. A couple of days before the dance I received a card in the mail. When I opened it a big heart popped out. It was from Jill. She apologized for not being able to spend time with me. She explained what happened with her family and they were planning to go away for a few days. She said when she came back she would make it up to me. Of course I was happy I was going to get my love back, but it didn't change that I was going to spend time with Kimberly until I did.

A week after the dance Jill called me over to her house. I thought, finally, we were going to see each other. I was excited. When I arrived to her house she handed me a box with anything and everything I had ever given her. Her sister answered the door and I could see Jill and her mother in the background. Jill came from a family where both parents lived in the home. Her father was very supportive of his wife and he did everything to protect his daughters. He hated that I got around the defenses and somehow got close enough to his daughter to hurt her. I honestly believe he chose not to be there when I came that day. I think he would have dealt with me the way a father would deal with someone like me. The way *I* would deal with someone like me. Her mother gave me a look that read, 'I wish I could support you, but you messed up.' Jill was crying. Not like the tears I'd seen Christmas day. The tears showed the pain I caused; the disappointment and the unanswered question of "why?"

This is where the evil that's in you flees. When having to face the light of justice, of cruel things you have done, the evil that's in you departs and what's left is emptiness. I didn't have answers. I just took the box, put my head down, and apologized. I turned away and walked down the stairs knowing that I had messed up. I got in my car and I went home. I was damaged. I was heartbroken because I was in love, but I didn't know how to let go of the lust. Sex had won the war at this point in my life. Sex had stolen from me all that love could've brought me. Sex held onto the heavyweight belt and became the undisputed champ in my life,

When young men are faced with sex and love they go through a gamut of feelings influenced by outside forces. It is so difficult for love to find a toehold that they'll make the same mistakes. They'll go through the motions of love, but they won't know how to sustain it because sex or evil can't be in the same place where righteousness and love are. It just can't happen. In one way or the other, one is going to stand on top. Each person has to decide for themselves which one it's going to be. If young men begin a sexual relationship with no influence on love then they won't fight for love.

Fathers, show your young men what it looks like to be respectful to a woman. Talk to these young men and explain to them what love really is. Love is not something that is so far out there that it's scary to talk about. It is not a sign of weakness to be humble and soft and romantic. It is not a negative to be in love. Explain that it takes bravery. It takes a man being more of a man to hold his ground and say this is the woman I love. This is the woman that I choose over any other woman out there. Teach them that that type of love should be the goal.

The Addiction

There's one thing I never considered throughout the years. What I had was a form of addiction when I really get to the heart of it. I placed myself at risk. I placed my loved ones at risk. I placed my significant others in past relationships and my current relationship in jeopardy because I took so many chances with my life.

I regret having been with over three hundred women in my lifetime. I know you're thinking how I came up with that number. It's pretty simple. My first sexual experience was at twelve years old. I wasn't monogamous until I got married three years ago. On average, I had sex with ten women per year. So if you're talking twenty-eight years there's your three hundred. If I throw in casual encounters that I may have forgotten it would probably be closer to four hundred.

My sexual escapades ranged from very common to surreal. When I look at the things that I would do to place myself around sex, I don't think you could call it anything, but an addiction high. When you get the opportunity to experience it, like any other drug, you want more. Throughout my life I attempted to have sexual encounters with almost every woman that I had conversation with. Even if I didn't express it to them, I thought about them sexually. Any woman that walked by me was a potential victim; old, young, white, black, tall short, and even physically impaired. No one was off limits. Just a glance at a face then the body and some sexual fantasy would run through my head.

I have even paid for sex. Yes, I have used prostitutes. I worked the midnight to eight shift at the front desk of a short-stay motel from 1988 until 1991. To put this into perspective this means customers paid to have a room for four hours, do whatever they wanted then left. The housekeeper would come, clean up the room and have it ready for the next occupant who was going to come and do the same thing. Most of the time people spent their time either getting high, having sex, or a combination of both. We even had individuals come to the hotel to use the rooms to prepare drugs to be sold on the streets.

Sometimes men and women were there with someone other than their spouses, and on many occasions you would find women there because they were selling their bodies for drugs or money. Basically everything that was going on in the streets was going on inside this motel. Because I worked the front desk it made it easier for me to know who was doing what and then offer what I had in exchange for sex. With my position I began to learn which women to stay away from, which women made it easier, and those I didn't have to offer money. I could offer them an extra hour or two to stay in a room. I could let them get a free room when they came back to make their money and that fed into my behaviors even more.

I had become a real pimp now. Never stopping to think what damage I was doing to myself physically and mentally. During the time I worked at the motel I was married to my first wife, but it didn't stop my antics. In my free time, when I wasn't working, it was always about the sexual escapades. Sometimes you get so caught up in that lifestyle that you believe it's the only way that things work.

People may think it's one of the lowest forms of sexual behavior, to pay for sex, but prostitution is one of the oldest professions in the world. The truth is more men have paid for sex than would likely admit it. It's especially easy when you meet a drug addicted woman who is still somewhat functional and hasn't quite lost her beauty. When you're around prostitutes and women who have done drugs and use their bodies to get drugs, you get used to a certain language. You get used to hearing little buzz words that tip you off that there might be a little something more than just a smile.

You don't have to take them out to dinner and a movie. You don't have to impress them, and they are less likely to discriminate. Prostitutes, especially those that do drugs, don't have patience or time to do much haggling or negotiation. So, you put it on the table what you want, what you have in exchange, and where the job will get done.

A lot of it is what you want to do? How do you want to do it? Where can we go and do it? And are you going to give me money to do it? You pretty much already know what that is. The question is now do you want to be bothered with this particular person? Also one thing to keep in mind when you do decide to get with a prostitute who's doing drugs is you're going to have to consider the fact that she is going to come back to see you once she knows that's a source of money for her. She's going to come back to see you even if you may not want her to come back because she doesn't have other sources of money. Many times prostitutes would show up to the hotel when I didn't want them.

When you start to pile it together there were so many opportunities that there was no reason to change my behavior until something forced me to. My mindset was the same for so many years because I continued to benefit in ways that a lot of people couldn't fathom. When you're an intelligent man or woman, you can convince others to just give in by becoming whatever they need you to become. I was a friend and I would use that friendship to work around defenses. I was a great listener so I would listen for the mistakes of other men and use that to my advantage. I was a romantic. I would use romance to wine and dine and cause women to want to be with me, but at the end of the day, what I was best was a liar. You can't be an addict of anything without being a great liar to yourself. I guess that's why when anyone asks, 'Do you think you were a sex addict during those days of running the streets?' I would always deny it because I didn't know that I was. I didn't believe that I was. I lied to myself so much and then I always had an answer for why I did what I did, and for how I treated people.

It has been really difficult to come face to face with what I was. The reality of it brings me to tears at times because I can't believe that that person was me. As I use this format to purge I start to see how others saw me; the women that loved me, the women that hated me, even the women that didn't realize and still don't realize that they were just a pawn in my game. The sad thing through it all there was no love.

Abortions & Miscarriages

A responsible man will take the necessary precautions to avoid many of the mistakes I made, but because I was not that man I did everything I could to not be held accountable for my actions. When I first decided to write my story I had to decide how much of me I was going to reveal. The number of pregnancies I had a hand in, that ended in abortions and miscarriages, I am not proud of. It's also a topic I tend to avoid when I do public speaking because it is one of the most emotional aspects of my life. Even now as I write it is difficult for me to decide on how to present it. So I figured the only way to do it is to be straightforward.

If I really took time to come up with an exact number I have contributed to possibly thirty pregnancies that resulted in either miscarriage or abortion. The truth is I don't know the number because I didn't care to keep count. When women became pregnant I was good at convincing them not to have a baby with me. I told them I would be the worst father in the world. Little did I realize, at the time, I was telling the truth. I would play on the circumstances of any situation. I'd tell women "We can't have a baby because we haven't finished school yet", "You don't want to have a baby right now because we don't have jobs, and we still live with our parents." In some cases I even threatened women into having abortions. Whatever it took I did not want to be held down with a baby. When women I slept with had miscarriages I felt like the luckiest man in the world. That meant it was one less trip to the abortion clinic pretending to be a concerned boyfriend. I wasn't prepared to be a father so after I was assured that the situation was taken care of I would breathe a sigh of relief and move on to the next conquest. Do you know how cold your heart has to be to take enjoyment in someone losing a child?

After the breakup with Jill, Kimberly and I continued to see each other for no other reason except that Kimberly was there. I remember walking through school and one of Kimberly's friends walking over to me.

"I heard. Congratulations", she looked at me with this big smile.

My confusion turned to anger when they started to explain that Kimberly told them she was pregnant. I was angry because I didn't understand why she would tell her friends before she would tell me. Then I was angrier because I was used to keeping these situations a secret until I could convince the women to terminate the pregnancies. Usually they would be too ashamed about what they did to tell anyone that they were ever pregnant.

I went into panic mode. She'd told more than one friend. Did this mean she was thinking about keeping the baby? I couldn't have that. I had already started going through my rolodex of pre-rehearsed anti-baby speeches. When I finally got a chance to see Kimberly I was disgruntled and obnoxious. I tried to become her worst nightmare. I wanted her to be so unhappy that she wouldn't even consider having my baby. When it didn't seem to be working I went into utter disrespect mode.

"Well, how do I know that this baby is even mine?" I went right for the jugular. I fired back with words many men use, but most don't consider the damage it causes. "If you have this baby, I won't have nothing to do with you or the baby. You need to choose what you want. Do you want me or the baby?"

Players will try to turn the situation around to their advantage. They will use a woman's emotion about the situation and play directly to that by making it seem as if you make this choice, you lose me which is the worst thing a man can do because there is no reason to place a woman in that situation when you've already created the foolishness. It didn't make any sense, but it was my only weapon. If this game was going to work to my advantage I needed to really go all the way with it. So, I really turned on the negativity. Once I had broken Kimberly down emotionally she gave in.

"Fine, I don't want to have your baby. I don't want to have anything to do with you."

Days later I was hanging out with a friend. I was telling him about the situation with Kimberly and how I was happy she decided not to have the baby. Like I mentioned earlier most of the time when you know a stupid guy he has stupid friends that fuel his foolishness. He asked me, "How do you know she really had the abortion?" Now I had a sick feeling in my stomach. He continued, "You know women lie and she can be sitting around pregnant right now and you could turn out to be a father later."

I decided to pay Kimberly a visit the day of her appointment to terminate the pregnancy. She looked tired and she was clearly in pain. I could see it on her face. The more I think about it, the more it hurts to know I placed women in that situation so many times. A sensible person would have shown some concern and compassion, but this wasn't about her. This was about me. All I was concerned about was whether or not she did what she was supposed to do.

I made small talk as she laid on the couch. "Well, how did things go?"

"It went okay. Everything is taken care of."

"Yea, but how do I know that?" I asked her with the most insensitivity anyone could fathom, but hey it went along with the territory. Most men who are sleeping with multiple women do not have the compassion needed in this type of situation and if they show any care at all you can believe it is not sincere. They just fake the sensitivity very well to get what they want.

I could see the anger on her face. "Fine, I'll show you." Kimberly walked away from me, and went into a back room. When she returned she handed me a receipt. The top of the receipt had the name and address of the clinic. Below it read in bold letters 'TOP.' In my ultimate stupidity, I asked, "What is TOP? You went to have an abortion. What does TOP mean? This doesn't make any sense. How come it doesn't say, 'abortion'?"

In a very loud and painful voice she screamed, "TERMINATION OF PREGNANCY YOU ASSHOLE!"

I could see the tears forming in her eyes and I just looked dumbfounded as I handed her back the receipt and she snatched it from me. She then asked me to leave her house. I did.

I'm not going to go through every single episode, but all of them ended in similar scenarios. It wasn't until I was older, more mature, and more experienced that I started to think about the toll it took on each woman. I had the nerve to ask women to make a choice that could be so detrimental because I wasn't ready to be a man. Without any regard I chose to end many lives simply because it made things easier for me. It's tragic that many of those choices resulted in devastating circumstances.

Many years later I ran into Kimberly on the street. To my surprise she no longer had any ill feelings toward me and I didn't end up at the end of a knife in my chest. We talked for a bit and when I asked if she had any children she told me that she would never be able to have children as a result of the abortion. I cannot stress it enough, but the weight of knowing that I altered someone's ability to have children weighs heavily on me. I now wonder how I lived my life the way I did without conscience. Until I gained a certain level of comfort with myself, I didn't gain an understanding of what my future might be and what my role is on this planet. Men must learn to respect themselves and, therefore, respect the women that they choose to be with. Until we achieve a level of self-respect, we will continue to make poor and harmful decisions that affect ourselves and others.

Towards the end of my first marriage things grew very negative; we were very unhappy with each other. Barely spending time together and making what I termed "marital service calls". We would go several months without any intimacy. It hit home that we barely had any physical contact when, one day, my son asked, "Why Don't you and Mommy hug like...?" I realized this was no way for children to see their parents interact with each other. Our marriage lacked emotion, love, and nurturing that is supposed to take place between a husband and wife.

With two children with my ex-wife we were already spread too thin. So when she announced that she was pregnant again, I knew we were not financially, emotionally, romantically, or spiritually in a position to have another child. We could not surgically terminate the pregnancy because early in our relationship, before we got married, she did it. A second surgical termination would put her health at risk. However, we came to terms that having a third child was not possible so we found a clinic that offered an experimental drug: RU486.

My ex-wife was one of the first women in New York City to go through this study. We went through the counseling process and received all of the information that was available about RU-486. I was very callous about the whole situation. I wasn't concerned that the drug was still experimental or what complications it might cause. I was only concerned with ending the pregnancy.

After taking the medication she began to experience discomfort yet I did nothing to ease her pain. I didn't hold her or let her know I was there for her. I didn't tell her everything would be all right. I simply tuned her out. I remember sitting there and having absolutely no connection to her during what I now realize can be a traumatic experience. It wasn't like when you go into the clinic and the doctor gives a women anesthesia then she wakes up and everything is all done. In contrast, when women take RU-486 your body reacts similar to child birth. The uterus contracts in order to expel the fetus and causes almost as much pain as delivering a full-term baby. I didn't understand this at that time, but it was obvious she was hurting. Incredibly, I was more annoyed that I had to hear her complaints. What kind of man was I to sit there and basically just wait for the process to take care of itself? I don't expect her to ever forgive me.

vNot too long after, while being unfaithful, I created a child with another woman who I couldn't convince to go through the same trauma. Here I was worried about taking care of a third child within my marriage and now I was being forced to do so outside of it.

My ex-wife and I were divorced when she found out about the child I had while we were still married, but it didn't take away her pain. I have since apologized many times to her for what I put her through, but I know I can't say I am sorry enough to make up for it. I know she doesn't accept it and I don't blame her. This is why I continue to ask God to forgive me. I pray that someday she'll find it in her heart to forgive me just so that pain is gone.

I always say no sin goes unpunished. Now, I'm in a wonderful and mutually supportive marriage. Tiffany and I experienced the loss of a child five years ago, and unfortunately have not been able to conceive since. I don't think it is what the Lord wants for us right now and that's something that I have to deal with. Tiffany came into a ready-made family with six children so we are considering adopting a baby or two. She actually wants five. We'd like to start a family that begins with love and not lust and infatuation. If the Lord sees fit for us to have children, then there would be no greater blessing, but it hurts to know that I am finally ready to create a family in a loving relationship, and can't do so. It's a painful realization, but I have come to terms that part of the repayment for my sins may mean I will never have a biological child with my wife.

If you have a man in your life whether it's your son, brother, boyfriend, uncle, or just a friend that finds pride, humor, and status in sleeping with multiple women and creating children haphazardly then there needs to be an intervention. A man can never understand what it is like to have life inside of you or the process from carrying a child to becoming a mother and what bonds are formed.

Men need to take ownership of their actions and the results of them. Right now I am using myself as an example. I have opened up myself to ridicule because I want this cycle to stop. Men are aiding in the breakdown of the family structure. I hope by putting myself on display other men will begin to see the damage they area doing and make changes.

Many have told me it was a blessing that those children weren't born because it would have just been a phenomenal mistake to have so many children running around the world with a father like me. Where I am in my life, spiritually, I would rather be the father of thirty children than the murderer of one. It disturbs me that abortion is used as a matter of convenience. We conveniently have casual and irresponsible relationships then we tell ourselves we can't be inconvenienced by the results of the casual choices we make. How selfish is that? Where I once believed that I had no other options I realize now that the Lord is the only option. He will provide for you. It may be tough, but that is a part of life. People may wonder am I a convert to pro-Life now. You don't have to wonder. The answer is yes.

As I end this chapter of my life, I beg you to not place yourself in a situation where you are forced to make the decision between life and death. What I lost was far greater than what I gained. Understand the consequences that may come from your actions. You may be damaging yourself or someone else for the rest of your lives. It's embarrassing to think how foolish I acted. I regret having lived that way, but it was who I was.

Being Married (The First Time)

When I have speaking engagements I talk tremendously about my current marriage, but I don't tend to mention anything much about my first other than there was one. I wasn't sure if I was going to discuss it in this book because there are so many emotions connected to the experience that I did not think I wanted to revisit it. Everyone who gets married does it with their individual beliefs of what they think marriage is. Once you have spent time, energy, blood, sweat, and tears trying to maintain it you realize that it's totally something different than when you first went in.

My first marriage was probably like most marriages going through similar trials, but my sexual behaviors and lack of care for the marriage must have attributed to its demise. My first wife and I met, in college, in 1985. We became friends first running in the same circles at school. Over a period of four years we spent enough time hanging out that we began to like each other. Of course I was attracted to Mica and made my move on her from time to time, to no avail. She was very strong willed and she didn't take any nonsense. The one thing I've learned over the years is that women who have back bone seem to pique my interest more because being the spoiled man that I had become; it was hard for me to take no for an answer. What I would find though is that usually when women told me "no" it wasn't no you can't have it, but usually no you can't have it, right now. This meant I had to figure out what I needed to do in order to get it.

Obviously, I got past those defenses in order to be able to have this chapter of the book, but it wasn't easy. Once Mica gave in to dating me I started to convince myself that I was ready to settle down. I knew Mica wasn't going to put up with any of my foolishness and she definitely was too headstrong for the mind games that I played with other women. So, I started to show her the other side of me; the emotional, nurturing, and romantic man that I could be. Like most of my previous relationships it started out sexually-based, but we also enjoyed each other's company.

I'll honestly say that during this time my relationship with Mica was exclusive. After the first eight months of our relationship we decided to introduce each other to our respective families. Like I mentioned earlier my mother and grandmother never had much to say about the women I brought around. They probably understood that those previous girlfriends were "just for now" or the main one of many. Though they were always respectful, but didn't make a big deal that I was in another relationship.

When it was time for me to meet Mica's mother on the other hand it was a different experience. Mica inherited her strong will from her mother. I can still remember this five foot four Haitian woman walking into the room and commanding it. Dignity was written all over her face. She knew exactly what she wanted to say, she was going to say it, and not make any excuses about it. She gave me a stern look as if she wanted to make sure I understood what she was about to say. I introduced myself and sat down.

"You have a drink with me?" she asked   She reached for two wine glasses and began pouring a bottle of rum. This was the first time that a girlfriend's mother offered me something other than water or a soft drink so I was a little confused, but I also didn't want to be rude. She held up her glass and I returned the salute. As a college student I had my share of drinking experiences, but this was the strongest drink I ever had. It burned going down my throat and left me choking and gasping for air. At the same time I watched this older women take her glass of rum down like she was drinking water.

Mica's mother explained to me what my role as her daughter's boyfriend had better be and what she expected. I never had someone's mother or father lay down the law like that before. This was the first time that someone actually said, "This is how I want you to treat my child. Honestly, I believe more parents need to have that type of discussion with the boyfriends and girlfriends their children choose. Most people think it should be automatic that any parent is concerned about the well-being of their child, of course, but there is a difference when that parent verbalizes it directly to you. It feels almost like a threat. It was like her mother was saying to me, 'You don't want to have to deal with me.' I respected Mica's mother for laying down the law.

Ironically, as luck would have it, about a week after that meeting I received a call from a friend. He told me he ran into Dina who now had a baby that looked just like me. He said, "You better find out if that's yours."

Dina and I had been together only one time and when she told me she was pregnant we both were left with the understanding that she would have an abortion. When I called Dina to ask her about the baby she told me she did have a baby four months ago, but it wasn't mine. So I thought, cool, I dodged a bullet. Believe it or not, though, my ego got the best of me when I started doing the math and came to the conclusion that if I wasn't the father that meant she had to be cheating when we were together. You would think what difference it would make if I was rolling around with every woman I could find, but it made enough of a difference that I called Dina back and questioned her about it. Her response was, "We need to talk." This was my welcome to fatherhood.

Something I had been trying to avoid for the past ten years was now being dumped in my lap and I wasn't ready to deal with it. I was finally in a relationship that meant a little bit more to me and now I am being faced with having to tell my girlfriend that I have a child.

Mica was extremely upset and her response was a prelude to what our future would hold. In hindsight, I should have paid more attention to it. When I explained it to my current wife, Tiffany, she said something that made so much sense. Often, she says, 'In a relationship, a person is going to show you either by accident or on purpose who they really are. At that point you're going to make a choice in a split second to acknowledge it and deal with it or see it and ignore it, but either way the person is going to show you.' I have to believe that she is right on.

I remember calling Mica with a mixture of emotions. "You're never going to believe this," I paused, "I just found out that I'm a father." What came next I wasn't prepared for. At that moment of my life the woman I was falling in love with went on a tirade of accusations and assumptions. I was already broken emotionally and Mica stripped me of any existence of hope. She never asked me any details like how, what, when, why? She chastised me then hung up. I couldn't understand why she was so angry with me as if I had betrayed her. Well, it didn't get any better when her mother also called and concluded that I was a liar, I knew about this child, and I basically put her daughter in a negative situation. Mica and I broke up.

For four months I felt empty. I didn't have my girlfriend anymore, and I wasn't ready to be a father. My mother, God bless her, truly understood because she had already been through a whole lot when it came to men. With three children by three different men she said to me, "You don't have to chase anybody around. Just be a father to your child. Just be the father that your father wasn't to you." I couldn't accept that I didn't know how to be a father. I saw my daughter as an interruption to my life especially because it cost me my relationship with Mica. If anything I was a horrible father.

When I went to Dina's house to see my daughter it was only for a couple of hours at a time. I used my leverage with being the baby's father in order to have sex with Dina when I wanted to. The only time I took my daughter out of her mother's house was to take her to my mother and grandmother's house and they were going to do everything they could that would foster me not having to be a real father. Not intentionally, but because I had allowed myself to be portrayed as the unwilling victim in this circumstance it was easy to play on their emotions instead of them just kicking me in the butt and saying to me, "Be a man." It got to the point that I think I enjoyed going to the house to have sex more than to be a father. Dina was living with her parents at the time and they did not like me. I can understand now it was justifiable. I would try to come to the house when they weren't there just so I didn't have to feel uncomfortable being around them.

Three months after breaking up Mica and I decided to get back together. You'd think I would have appreciated that she accepted me back and I would do everything I could to make sure that our relationship was solid. No. Instead, I was juggling girlfriend and baby mama for a while until eventually I stopped having sex with my daughter's mother. Once we stopped having sex the less time I spent with my daughter. Although I made sure that my daughter's mother was receiving financial support I wasn't really stepping up to responsibility and Mica was indifferent to the time I spent with my daughter.

Something else my current wife brought to my attention. Why would any women want to be with or love a man that shows no love or nurturing for his own child? You find a man that has several children with several different women and then has no consistent relationship with his children you shouldn't want anything to do with him. Too many women allow men in their lives to use simple reasons to explain their non-relationships with their children. Unless a man can show you judicial documentation for a reason he has no contact with his children then you should wonder are his excuses valid. Then again, if he provides you with a document that would prevent him from having contact with his children would you really want to be a part of that?

Some people have told me it was intentional, because of envy of my daughter, that a year after we reunited Mica got pregnant. All I can say is we were not using protection so she can't bare full responsibility for getting pregnant. We both already knew what the circumstances were so if either one of us wanted something different we would have taken the precautions to ensure we didn't end up with a baby. I remember sitting with my mom shaking my head because I couldn't believe where my life was spiraling. By this point I had been kicked out of college because I was failing in school, I was in a job that I didn't like, I had my daughter's mother who I was arguing with all of the time and couldn't see eye to eye, and I didn't have a relationship with my first child.

One day my mother asked me, "You don't have a clue what you're doing, do you?" I answered, "No, I don't. I never expected to be here." I had backed myself into a corner that I couldn't get out of because I wasn't putting my behavior in check. I was going after what I wanted instead of what I needed. Would you believe I was still having sex with other women besides Mica and Dina?

This was the second time my mother said to me "Just be a father." The Lord was speaking to me through my mother and I wasn't listening. When you have never been shown how to be a father where do you start? All my life I was shown how to be a pimp and get over on women. All the while I kept thinking to myself I didn't want to be like my father. Having children all over with different women and not doing anything for them. I thought getting married was the answer. So, in all honesty, I didn't get married out of love I got married because I felt obligated to. I knew my mother had been abandoned by the father's of all her children and I didn't want to be like them. I felt that if I got married, it was going to be the best thing in the world and things would get better.

Mica and I went to City Hall before my son was born. The process was so generic and lacked the deeper meaning of marriage. I walked through one door said, "I do." Then walked out of the building thinking, "Ok, I'm married now." This is not how I thought I would get married, but I also never thought I would be married. Actually, I remember wondering if this was what my life was going to be like; almost like a business arrangement. I remember turning to Mica and saying we're not going to do it like this. We have to do it the right way. Again, wanting something different, but not having a plan.

After my son was born in January 1992 we decided to have a big wedding. I can estimate between credit cards and money that should have been used on other things Mica's parents spent Fifteen to twenty thousand dollars on our second wedding which, at that time, would have been a sizeable down payment on a house. When I think about it we were already married what was the need for the pomp and circumstance? We didn't even have our own place. My wife, son, and I went back to live with my in-laws after wasting all of that money. I wouldn't know until years later that my wedding video would be the testament of what my marriage would be.

While living with my second wife we were cleaning out our apartment. Getting rid of old things, stuff we no longer used, and things that were just taking up space. I came across my wedding video in a box. Of course Tiffany, being the Wedding Network junky wanted to watch it. As we watched we laughed at the comical moments, we sighed at the momentous ones. Then it came time when the videographer wanted to get the parting words from the married couple. After I expressed my love, or at least what I thought was love, the videographer pans the camera to my bride. When it's time for her to say something wonderful about her husband the first words out of Mica's mouth were, "He gets on my nerves, but I love him." She then follows up the insult with, "and if it doesn't work out, I want my money back because my family is spending a fortune."

I had never seen the expression on Tiffany's face like the one she had that day. If she could have turned red she definitely would have. "I am so embarrassed for you right now," she said, "Who, in their right mind, insults their husband on their wedding video like that?" Tiffany was right. This was another instance where Mica had tipped her hand of her true character. Tiffany went on to restate what was said in the video, "You get on her nerves, and she wants her money back if the marriage doesn't work out?" Now that I think about it who talks about the amount of money they're laying out on their wedding video? I couldn't see it that day because I had been drinking so much and I was clowning with my friends and just having a good time. These are the things that if you pay close enough attention; the Lord will send you all the signs you need that you shouldn't be with someone. I was so screwed up; there was no way I was going to see the signs of anything other than what I wanted.

We didn't have money for a honeymoon so, I remember we went to Manhattan and reserved a nice hotel in Midtown for a couple of days. It just happened to be that it was that time of the month for her so we couldn't even consummate our marriage night as husband and wife. Instead we sat on the bed and I listened as my new wife criticized our gifts and cards.

She complained about the amounts of money my family gave in their cards; it wasn't enough according to her standards. Someone gave us a chicken fryer, or something. I thought it was a cool gift and I remember her going off about how corny the gift was and it's a shame that people don't know how to spend the proper money at a wedding. She even mentioned my family being ghetto and it was a waste of money inviting some of "those people" because of how they acted. I was sitting there thinking to myself, "I married this woman." Here it was, the day after my wedding and I'm regretting being married.

That evening we went to the movies to see "Menace to Society" and "What's Love Got to Do With It?" Its kinds of ironic that the first thing we saw as husband and wife was a movie about a man beating his wife. I remember when she went to sleep that night I went to look out of the window and was looking out over Manhattan. The skyline was beautiful. When you're up high you just see the movement of people and the cars. It's almost like a dance and everything looked so small. I remember feeling tremendously sad and saying to myself, "This is not how I pictured it. This is not how I expected things to be. What did I do to myself? Why did I let myself get here?" I wouldn't be able to share my feeling until many years later.

Two years later, not much had changed. We were still living with her parents and now she was about to have our second child. I'm going to interject something right here. Anyone who is planning on getting married, do not get married and have nowhere to live. Do not get married and your first home, as a married couple, is in either one of your parents' homes. Do not stay with your parents. You need to be completely autonomous of your parents because when you have disagreements or need to plan for your household and your new family it is a disadvantage to the other person when a spouse can run to mom's room or run to dad. It's a horrible feeling and no reason to start off your marriage that way.

So, when my second son was born and we were still living in her parent's house, I just grew tired. Her mother was exercising her will at different times because, of course, this was her house. We moved from one area of the house to another. We ended up in the basement where Mica's mother hired someone to renovate in order to make it livable. He did a horrible job, a lot of resources were wasted, and we didn't have the money to pay someone else to come in and fix it. Finally, we gathered ourselves together, got our finances in order, and we moved. We found an apartment in Canarsie, Brooklyn, and it was close enough that she could still be near her mom.

It wasn't until Mica and I were on our own, in our own place, that it started to become clearer that my marriage was not going to work. Everyone around me saw it, but didn't express that Mica was a dictator in our marriage. She'd say and I would do. Her mother was bossy and she was bossy and to just keep the peace while living in her mother's house I just went along to get along. I didn't express myself the way I wanted until I was around my friends and family. I almost felt stifled.

I learned, in the Haitian culture, women have a dominant role and the men will take a step back and pretty much just let things play out and speak when they need to speak and that's kind of it and the women are used to just doing what they want, to a point. I wasn't raised in a home like that. I wasn't raised that a man should stay quiet. The men that I saw with my mother and grandmother spoke their minds and as crazy as their behaviors were at times took a leadership role in the house. I had traditional southern parents who felt the man is the king of the castle and that's what he should actually be and that he should put his foot down when he needs to and everything should go through him.

I had been sucked into this vortex called Mica's world. I didn't spend much time with my own family. I didn't even bring my children to see my family regularly. I honestly believe it was from sheer embarrassment the way Mica would act when she was around my family that I just kept my distance. Mica's behavior was—now when I look at it—just disrespectful. If we were at a family gathering where meals were being served she would ask who cooked the food before eating as if she had to validate if it was okay for her to eat or not. She would also ask if certain foods tasted good, and would frown up her face. She made no attempt to be discreet and was often rude with her behavior. My friends and family tolerated her because they cared about me. I found out so much after our divorce that just wasn't said when I was married.

I always think about the times that I conceded when Mica would throw a virtual tantrum in order to have things her way in our relationship. There are so many times I regret not putting my foot down. For example, in 1991, when Mica was pregnant with our first son, I had an opportunity to have an all expense paid trip to Jamaica, West Indies. Someone had thought enough of me and my skills that I was asked to coach basketball there for the summer. It had been a life-long dream to coach basketball professionally.

When I came home with this exciting news the first thing Mica said was, "You're going to go to a Caribbean island and leave me? Are you crazy?" So, I didn't go. In 1992, after my son was born, I was asked to go to Jamaica because of my knowledge and my understanding of the game of basketball. Again I received no support from my wife. "You're going to leave me with the baby here to go and coach a game?" I said, "But this is something that I've dreamed about doing and they've asked me a second time for the second year. I should do this." Her response was, "So again, you're going to think about you and leave me and the baby here."

Again, I had to decline the offer. For a second year in a row the players came back to tell me how things went and how much my coaching skills were missed.

In 1994, when I graduated from Kingsborough Community College with my Associates Degree I was on the Honor Roll and was offered a partial scholarship for a new program that was beginning at New York University. I was to receive ten thousand dollars a year toward a twenty-two thousand dollar tuition. My professor told me he thought I would be an excellent candidate and suggested I take a student loan for the remaining tuition. When I happily presented the information to Mica, I was shot down "How are we going to afford to pay a $12,000 loan and if you're going to go for four years, that means we're going to owe $50,000. How are we going to pay that? I'm already in debt from the wedding." I tried to argue the point, "But a degree from NYU would allow me to do that and we would definitely be able to pay it back."

"I don't think that's going to be the case because then what if you leave and I'm here with nothing?" Again, money and the dissolution of our marriage was her platform.

I didn't fight it too much to go to NYU because I was also intimidated by the thought that I may not be able to compete with students on that level. So, instead I figured I would go back to York College where I started. I hit another Mica roadblock.

"Wait a minute. You've been working part time while going to school, you got your Associate's Degree, how come you don't go back to work full-time for the year and help me out and then go back to school?"

"Well, my plan was to go straight to the four-year school, do my additional two years, get my Bachelors Degree, and then I'll be straight."

Like usual, she whined and complained until I changed my plan. I put school on hold and didn't start in the Fall of 1994, as I planned. I worked for a year then re-enrolled in York College in the summer of 1995. I finally received my Bachelor's degree in

Education two years later. Unfortunately, the delay in completing my studies came at a price.

In the summer of 1996, I had a job interview at Trinity College High School, one of the most prestigious private schools in Manhattan. It was for a position as Head Coach of the basketball team. It would include workouts and practices at the renowned Basketball City in New York. There was a twenty-five game schedule which included two tournaments. When I met with the hiring manager during the interview we realized that this wasn't the first time we had met each other. It turned out that three years earlier, in New Jersey, we met at a function and had a great conversation about—what else—basketball. After the second interview I had pretty much sealed the deal. I came in for a third meeting and the hiring manager says, "We need you to coach as well as teach physical education so I'm going to need a copy of your license."

"I still have two more semesters to complete and I will have my degree in the spring."

"Well, we need someone that can start now." She spoke to the Director, she called me back and she said, "I'm sorry, but unfortunately we can only hire you as an Assistant Coach. We can give you a partial salary for the coaching job, but we need someone with a degree also because you won't be able to teach."

At that time, this was the biggest disappointment? My dream job was about to be handed to me, but my arms were too short to reach it. I couldn't help, but think if I didn't take the year off I would have had my degree in enough time to be qualified for the job.

Mica and I were so far apart by the time I graduated, but we were still playing house. For example we had saved up enough money to take a vacation though it was against my better judgment. Mica wanted to take a trip to Cancun which would have cost over four thousand dollars. I suggested to her that we pay off some bills so, for the first time, we were ahead instead of behind. Like always, I was met with opposition, "You've got to be kidding me. I've never been anywhere. Why can't we go?" I said, "Okay, but understand if we do this, we are going to be behind when we come back."

"No problem," she said.

So imagine my surprise at the argument that ensued when we got back from vacation and didn't have enough money to satisfy Mica. It was another event that really started me to think about ending the marriage.

I started to see the lack of respect, support, and love Mica had for me as her husband. Her idea of husband was someone to, blindly, fulfill her every need. She made me feel more like an unvalued employee than a hardworking husband. I know some of you may be reading this thinking, "But you were cheating the whole time!" You're right. I can't argue that, but are the women in the street supposed to make me feel more like a man than my own wife? In our marriage, Mica made me feel that every time I couldn't grant her wish I was worthless to her. This continued even after the divorce in reference to our children. I didn't feel like she was my helpmate like the Bible says your wife is supposed to be. I was her trophy to put on the shelf to brag to all her friends that she has a "husband". I was her virtual bank that seemed to always be on empty when she was ready to splurge.

The final straw was during my first day working for the New York Department of Education. I had finally secured a position for my new career and not just another dead end job. I had history, in other jobs, of being a rebel because I chose to champion other's causes and was always sticking my nose into other people's affairs in an effort to help.

Mica drove me to work that morning. As I was getting out of the car in front of my new school, I said, "I'll see you later, okay baby?" I remember it like it was yesterday. Mica looked me in the face like she was chastising one of our sons and asked, "Do you think you can keep your mouth shut so you don't get in trouble? So you can hold onto this job because we need the money?" I was really hurt. It wasn't "Congratulations", "Have a good day", or "We've been through so much and now we are going to get ahead". I responded, "You have a great day too, Love." I remember walking through the door saying to myself, "I'm done."

That year was also the year that I used the internet to just look for any type of activities to get involved in that were not connected to my marriage. I was so frustrated that I was going to do whatever I wanted to do with whomever I wanted. I didn't care anymore. I was using bowling as an excuse to get out of the house at night. Once I started working, I met some nice coworkers that were very cool to hang out with and we used to go out every Friday after work. A lot of teachers go out on Fridays to unwind from a long week. I would use Happy Hour to drink my sorrows away. I would drink until I was virtually blind and then I'd stagger home. It really didn't make a difference what Mica had to say because I was either too drunk to hear it or so tired that I would go collapse on the bed and we would just argue about it the next day.

I had repositioned my spot in the house from the master bedroom to the living room. We didn't sleep in bed together too often and lovemaking was next to nothing. If we did make love it was more as a service to each other simply because we were in the same house. When I think about it, I don't know if she cheated. I know I was cheating. She might have. I believe that she did, but it doesn't matter because she would have been well within her rights to cheat because I was emotionally detached. So, if she went out to find comfort in the arms of somebody else, it's not a shock to me and I would expect it because I pretty much drove her to that.

At that point my mission was to leave the house permanently. How could I achieve that? It started with a phone call from my mother the very next day. Someone from the New York City Department of Child Support Enforcement had called looking for me. When I called back I spoke to a gentleman on the phone who told me there was a case being brought against me for child support. I had them forward the documents to my mother's house and when I picked them up it was in reference to a young lady that I had been sleeping with off and on. She would be the second woman that would lie about having an abortion in order to have the baby. The only difference was I found out during the pregnancy she planned to have the baby and my son was now four months old.

When I showed up to the court house I shook my son's grandmother's hand and apologized that we had to meet under these circumstances. This was also the first time I held my son. I looked at him, I gave him back to the mother, and then I took my seat on the other side of the room. Karen knew I was married when we were together. She was one that I didn't wine and dine. I didn't try to impress her with trying to be a ladies' man. Her role was specific, although it was apparent that she wanted more. I honestly believe she thought by getting pregnant it would force me to have to be with her. She was sadly mistaken. That day in court, I requested a blood test that caused the mother of my son to become enraged. We argued and she decided she didn't want to have anything to do with me which made it better for me because the less I had to do with her, the less I had to do with the baby.

Approximately two months later I received the results that I was indeed the father of her child. I was going to have to pay child support. I had no problem with making sure that my children were provided for financially because I always believed if you created the child then you should make sure they are cared for. This child was the catalyst to me leaving my broken marriage.

When I told Mica I was leaving she did something I could not have suspected. Despite going through a loveless marriage for almost eight years, she cried and wanted to work it out. I knew there was nothing to work out. Unfortunately, I wasn't ready to go on the day I said I was ready to go. So, over the next four weeks we were enemies and until I finally moved out and back into my parents' house.

I was now laying in the same bed I had as a child. I couldn't believe that I was thirty-two-years-old and back home. My grandmother, God bless her, opened the door for me to come back home. We moved all of my stuff in and didn't even have a place to put it all. She opened my bedroom door as I sat there staring at the ceiling fan blades spinning around. She told me, "Cry tonight and then get your ass up because we didn't raise a soft man and you're going to make it no matter what the situation is. You're just going to be the father you need to be and no woman is going to break you." Some of the best advice I ever got.

To this day, I don't think Mica and I will ever be able to repair anything that would resemble a cordial relationship between us. Our children are the only reason why we converse with each other and if we didn't have children, we probably wouldn't speak at all. Still, I acknowledge that the destruction of my marriage was not completely Mica's fault. I had a share in it. Part of my fault was coming to the table saying that I loved her when I didn't. Saying I wanted to marry her when I wasn't sure. Trying to be a husband when I had no clue. Making babies that I wasn't able to take care of. Not being able to provide emotional, financial, romantic, and spiritual stability. I wasn't able to offer her anything while slowly taking from her so much that I left her empty of any possible positive feelings towards me.

Now, the only thing I can hope to happen, to make things better is for the Lord to step directly into her life and open her eyes to what the world could be through Him. I don't believe that anything I do for her in any way is going to make things remotely positive because of what I've done to her.

I want to take this moment to, publicly, apologize to Mica for the person I was. For all the pain I caused you, for not being anywhere near the husband I was supposed to be, for being deceitful, for being so emotionally distant. I allowed myself and other women to trample on what should have been our sacred marital bed, and for allowing my anger and disappointment in myself to be displaced towards you. I have since released my anger. The Lord has stepped in to heal me, and I pray the same for you with the hope that you'll find peace.

As I bring this chapter to a close, I want to address friends of people who are being unfaithful. We need to stop being afraid to speak up and say, "What you're doing is wrong." I have learned firsthand that you can't be neutral when it comes to infidelity. Either you are in support of infidelity or you are not. To attempt to show indifference is a lack of care and respect for your friend and their spouse.

I ask those considering marriage to take a step back and understand that marriage is a commitment which is life-altering. Each person has to come into it with the idea that there has to be mutual sacrifices. One shouldn't come away feeling like they have made all the concessions for the sake of the marriage.

I also ask that if you are married and are having an affair or considering having one think about what you are taking away from your spouse and children. Men can believe they are being a good father, but any moment you take to be with your mistress is a moment that cannot be given back to your children. If your marriage is such that you need to seek comfort with other women than either there needs to be more communicated to your wife or you need to consider why you are in the marriage.

Big Beautiful Women & The Internet

There's a point in every man's life when he finds a particular activity to fill his free time; something that entertains him and keeps his attention for long periods of time. For some men it can be the local bar. It could be the pool hall, golf, watching sports on television, or even playing cards. My activities were mostly centered around wherever plus sized women would be. I have always been an outgoing and sociable person with the ability to meet women anywhere, but one thing I can say is when I stumbled upon the BBW world I was like a piranha. BBW is the acronym for Big Beautiful Women and there's a whole society out there full of BBW and the people who love them.

The BBW community consists of smaller organizations that plan various events geared toward plus sized women. This includes parties, shows, vacations, shopping, and whatever anyone can think of to get BBWs together. The BBW community is the most lucrative environment I could have been in order to fill my appetite. It is full of women that society constantly bombards with the idea that they are not sexy and shouldn't like themselves. Women who go into public places and hope they have seats that will accommodate their size. Women who go into a party or a club to have a great time like everyone else and then get treated like exhibits at the zoo with people staring, pointing, and even laughing. So, big beautiful women and their admirers decided to create their own venues that they felt comfortable in.

You can find a BBW event in pretty much most of the major cities now, but in 1989 when I came across my first BBW Party it was more like a secret club. My friends and I were traveling to Manhattan to go to a strip club every week. I would notice these BBWs going into a club on 44th Street and 8th Avenue in Manhattan. One night, I decided to stop and meet BBWs from every bit of the spectrum: tall, short, black, white, and every shape you could imagine. Believe it or not the only problem I had with going that night was that so many of them were overtly promiscuous. Yes, I know I'm a hypocrite, and yes there is a double standard. I could sleep with as many women as I wanted to, but as soon as I found out the woman I liked was loose I didn't want anything to do with her. So, I never returned to the club.

It wasn't until 1997, after cruising Yahoo! Clubs on the internet that I came across more BBW clubs. They all had individual sites that catered to whatever types of BBW you were attracted to. Mostly all the sites had one thing in common though. Club Peppers. It seemed to be the most happening place for BBWs. They held monthly events and it was a magnet for every woman of size that had an internet connection. The first night I went there were wall to wall women. It was like the wolf being allowed to party with the chickens. How long is he going let his food sit around before he eats?

I exchanged numbers with about three or four women that night. Peppers became my stomping grounds. Having a club where I knew I would find new potential victims every time I went and then having the internet as a means to be able to reach them whenever I wanted, even with my wife in the next room I had basically found a never-ending source of sexual satisfaction. My wife had no concept of how to work the computer so I was able to hide files and pictures all over.

After about a year, as my marriage continued to plummet, my connection to the BBW community soared. I started wearing my wedding band on a gold chain around my neck. It was a great way to pretend to be the disheartened husband in an unloving marriage. When my first wife stopped wearing her band she gave it back to me. It just made my story stronger when I added her band to the chain and would say that we were separated. Playing my role as the unhappily married man I would say, "I'm not looking for a real relationship because I just got out of a failed marriage." I would show the two rings on the chain, "You see, this is my wife's wedding band around my neck. It just didn't work. I don't want anything serious because I don't trust anybody right now."

All a man has to do is look vulnerable and be fairly attractive and he's in a good place. Meanwhile, women have this need to be a man's savior. So I just pretended I needed someone to save me from my sorrow of being in a failed relationship. They never asked was I the cause of my failed marriage.

When I started to learn about other organizations that branched out and started to cover areas in New Jersey and Philadelphia my infidelity was out of control. I was having sex two or three times a week. My wife actually believed that I was unable to perform because we would go months without ever touching each other. I didn't care that I wasn't having sex with my wife because it conserved my energy for the different women I met at the clubs.

Once you're connected to this underbelly of vileness, you now start to find new sets of BBW groups on the internet that are nastier than the ones that you were a part of before. Private groups would allow you to become a member because they've seen you at the parties, they've danced with you, they've talked with you, and they say 'Join my group' and before you know it you're in. Once you are in you get to see all types of things people would never put out in the open. I started to meet women from around the country. I was drunk on women and I couldn't get enough.

Two strong years of this activity and now I was moving into another one of the well-known organizations, BABs: Big And Beautiful. The BABS organization was based in New Jersey. They took BBW events to a whole different level when they started promoting full weekend events. You no longer had just one night to try to make your mark. Now, BABS made it so that you left all your inhibitions at home and for two and a half days, you acted as if the word didn't exist because you just partied, drank, and had sex pretty much all weekend long. From Friday to Sunday, sometimes Monday if it was a holiday weekend, you could have sex with as many women that had come on the trip if you played your cards right.

My friends and I found another level. I thought I had mastered everything, but like a game of chess, when the opponent changes and he brings a higher skill level, it then forces you to enhance your game. I was presented with weekend challenges. How could I not come away with having sex with as many women as I wanted when I was in a hotel, alcohol was flowing like water, and with women who had no inhibitions? These women would basically let you do anything as long as you made them feel special. It got to the point that I no longer had to pay for my trips. If I told a BBW I couldn't make it to the next event because I didn't have the money, even if I did, they would pay for my trip. Then as long as I performed my duties with them while I was there they didn't care who else I was having my fill with.

I know you're reading and thinking how stupid can these women be. It's not a matter of intelligence, but more about the desire to have someone in their lives. These women were happy to finally have someone interested in them and have their bodies appreciated; the opportunities were endless for me. The lady who paid for my trip was satisfied and I was satisfied. Then I didn't have to worry about her wanting to get serious because I already let her know that I wasn't ready because of my status. She couldn't come back to me and say, 'You know it's really messed up that you didn't want to get serious.' I was taking advantage of women who had emptiness and I was there to fill the void. It was a simple game for me and it fed my greediness. Big beautiful woman have always provided me with a forum because they have so much stacked against them that they allow themselves to endure almost anything hoping to find that man that they can call their own.

These parties created the scenario that allowed the wolf to run around unabated. I hate to say this because there are going to be women who attend those parties, and are going to be offended. If I have offended you, I'm sorry, but you make it so much easier for men like me to do the things that we do.

In these circles, women sleep with men who they are not physically attracted to, but because the men prefer plus sized women, they date them anyway. Also, men who may have never really had options can now run through as many women who are fine with "Mr. Right Now".

However, when a real good-looking man comes into the circle the competition is unfathomable. The skullduggery that takes place between friends, foes, and even sometimes family is unconscionable. I have actually sat and watched women plot how they can make the next woman look bad so she can move into a better position, but no one stopped to check if this man is worth the effort or drama. No one is checking if he actually came into this environment with good intentions. No one is actually holding the man accountable for his actions so if he comes in with any type of secret agenda, other women are assisting him in being that. Wars erupted and alliances formed. "Girl, I'm going to help you get that man because I don't like her anyway." At the same time the one that is "helping" you is plotting against you just so she can get closer to "that man" and getting him from right under your nose. This goes on on a regular basis. So, if you're offended because this doesn't apply to you then you need to check your friends.

Eventually, the BBW environment started to take its toll on me emotionally and physically. I was gaining weight because in those environments, it doesn't make a difference what size you are as long as you can perform. People would still say, "Hey, you look good!"

My partner, who came to the events with me, and I would look at pictures from when we first started going to the parties. The two of us had put on at least thirty to fifty pounds each because all you were doing was partying, eating, and drinking. When I look at the women I have met since I first started they have put on fifty to one-hundred pounds. You look at their pictures over the years and they are gradually getting bigger. No one cares that the lifestyle is now making you unhealthy. As long as you find someone that you can sleep with everything is all good in this big fantastic fairytale.

Becoming a Father

I recognize now my misogynistic attitude was a reflection of the hatred I had for myself and was fostered by the hate I had for my absent father. I hated him for not being there for me, and I took it out on the women around me. So, that self-hate was pushed out into the world into such a degree that I became self-destructive and acted in ways that were just brutal. Understand when you look at situations it's very subtle, at first, but grows into something tremendous.

For a good portion of my life, as a young man, I wanted my father to come into my life and be a part of it. Standing by as I learned to ride my bike for the first time. Teaching me how to hold the bat when I was learning to play baseball, Giving me pointers when I made the basketball and football teams, challenging me to a race—knowing I wouldn't be able to win until I got older, but just the sheer drive of wanting to beat my dad would have been enough. As I got older that desire to have my father vanished. It was replaced with anger that he wasn't there and a stronger feeling of not needing him in my life.

Mothers have an anchoring position here. They can actually foster the foolishness, which is often done when single mothers express they are the mother and the father of their children. You can be a very strong mother to your child, but you can never be the father they need.

A mother can also curb certain behaviors by letting her son know despite having an absent father there are still expectations and standards for him as he becomes a man. By doing the best she can to curb it, the mother cuts down on a lot of what this young man could possibly become as a result of not having a male role model. She may not be able to change it completely, however in many cases she can help guide him.

With myself, my mother never discredited the men in her life. She never treated our fathers with disrespect. She would just tell us straight-with-no-chaser: "They left, they didn't care, but we have each other." I think my pain was compounded by the fact that my sister's father had an opportunity to take over when my father failed. He abandoned us also. So growing up I had an example of two men shirking responsibility. It's no one wonder that when I became a father I repeated the pattern. I realize now that I had no respect for myself because I had no respect for the men that were in and out of my life. They taught me to be just like them.

People often ask if, 'If you knew you were not ready to have a child than why didn't you use protection?' Well, the first reason is pretty obvious so I won't go into that, but when you come from an economically lower class community you don't have much so you begin to create ways to find honor and value for yourself. Even though you may not have the means to take care of the child, just the mere fact that you created one gets you a pat on the back from your homeys. You're a real man now because you have planted your seed. The women bearing your babies are trophies on your shelf.

An out-of-control man takes pride in having multiple kids he can't take care of because that means he had multiple women that thought enough of him to make him "the man". It's a twisted way of thinking, but it's just as bad as a woman who thinks having a baby with a man is going to make him change for better or make him not want to be with anyone else because she has his baby.

Another reason—I don't thinks it's one that a lot of men are conscious of, but I believe it's high on the list—is that they secretly want a child. As a man you hope that things will be good when the baby arrives. However, if you've never had a man to show you how to be a man and never had a father to show you how to be a father, then how do you fulfill those roles?

My mother and grandmother are traditional southern mothers. So, when I told them I was a father, they knew it was going to happen. In their minds it was just another child that they we're going to accept into the family. You've seen this scenario on television and in films where the promiscuous African-American father has multiple children and the mother just takes care of the home regardless. My mother and grandmother were that way. They knew what their son and grandson was and they just simply said, 'As they come in, we'll take care of them.'

When I flashback to twenty years ago, I made tremendous mistakes. My daughter should have been paramount. She should have been enough to pull me out of what I was. My daughter should have been my single-minded focus in how I was going to live my life from that point on, but I just put her in line with the rest of the women I was out abusing and not surprisingly, she got abused because I was not there. Yes, I was providing financial support and I made sure my job put her on my medical benefits. In my mind, I had done a lot more than my father did for me. In fact, I would take offense to any comment that was made about me as if I wasn't a good dad, but I wasn't there.

The Lord asks from us to give to others. It is in the treatment of others that we're actually becoming what the Lord wants us to become. As a follower of Jesus Christ, I understand why He gave so much even though He had the power to take care of anything that He wanted. He gave of himself because it was a way to get people to understand what true love is. For people, it's easier to just want for yourself and be self-centered. It is very difficult to give to others without guarantee of getting anything. I started to understand I should have given so much more of myself to my daughter. I didn't and had a daughter that was growing without her father.

Her grandfather—her mother's father—was more of a father to my daughter than I could have ever even thought of being. That was a lost opportunity. Instead of possibly learning how to be a father from him I was comfortable with passing my role to him. I never thought that that man would lead my daughter in a direction that would be opposite what I was which would only cause more tension between the two of us.

If another man is raising your child and you have not stepped up to own that responsibility, don't be shocked if you see your child heading off in a direction that does not include you. Yes, he or she may acknowledge you as the biological father, but you will hear things like "My real father is...", "The man that raised me...", "The man that loved me...". If you are allowing another man to raise your child you have forfeited one of the most precious gifts in life. I can tell you it's like having an irreparable hole in your heart.

Even so, it is never too late to reclaim your right. That doesn't mean to force your way into someone's relationship. It means work along with the mother, stepfather, or whomever else has taken a parenting role. Become an active participant in your child's life. Take the time that you have with the child and make it your own. Not you and the fellas and your son or daughter—just you and your child.

Create a positive environment when they're with you. Have them participate in rites of passage with you. Then allow them to see and meet the people around you. Make a commitment to mentoring. Make a commitment to take them to events where they're going to see growth. This means you're going to have to put you to the side. It can no longer be about you.

I think the most important thing is to introduce your child to God. If you don't know God, use this opportunity as a chance for you to get closer to Him and allow your child to see that growth and be included. These are the situations and events that spirituality and faith play a major role in. Faith allows you to say, "Please help me be a better father." As you grow in your faith and understanding of your responsibilities you start to take more of an authoritative role in your child's life instead of a spectator. That's what the power of faith is.

For me, it is my belief in Jesus Christ who is my God. When I read the Bible I look to it for answers and guidance as a way to be able to function to gain the control I need over difficult situations.

If faith in the Lord is not for you, there are still ways to regain your child's trust and love which requires active commitment.

My hope is that you understand the choices we make have devastating consequences to our future and the futures of those we are connected to. In the last five years, I have started to realize the damage and devastation of my actions. I have to live with the pain of knowing what I put into motion. There are some quiet times when I am alone I become emotional, and I close my eyes and pray to get through. As an educator, I push very hard in the classroom and in school to try to be an example to the students I have today. It is my way of trying to make up for some of what I have done.

Becoming a father is such a wonderful gift that if you don't stop and consider the ramifications of misusing this gift, you will never truly be happy. If you have children out there that you are not connected to, you will never truly find the peace that you need. I don't care how happy you think you are. Because there is a child out there with your blood coursing through their veins they need a connection to their father who will listen and talk to them. Some of your mannerisms, some of your physical characteristics, some of your genes and chromosomes are in that child so some of your hang ups and some of your positives are also in that child. If you understand who you are then you may be able to help that child or your children how to deal with the things that they're having problems with.

It's also a way to give back if you have destroyed a part of this world in your actions and behavior. Through your children, you have a way of trying to repair the damage done. You may not be able to do it all yourself, but if you can curb your legacy, stop this negative train from leaving the station; you might have protected and saved future generations.

The Motel

Previously, I explained that I worked in a short stay motel for approximately four years. I think in everyone's life you have an opportunity to go back and analyze different places and situations you were in. Some people call them crossroads, some call them turning points. Either way they're times in your life where decisions you've made have a lasting effect on the rest of your life—the motel was one of those times.

I like to break things down into segments. I look at the different segments of my life to analyze where I was mentally and emotionally and try to figure out what could have happened if I had done things differently.

When I started working at the motel in Jamaica, Queens in 1988, I was driving cars for a major car rental company and had been involved in a really bad accident. I had to find something else to do. The opportunity to work at a motel in the neighborhood I grew up in just seemed to come at the right time. It was the perfect job in a local arena that fed right into my destructive behaviors. I was smack dab in an environment where people's sole reason for entering was to have sex. Some people would say, "Ok so what? It's your job. All you had to do was go to work, do what you were told to do and come home"—which was very true. However, I don't always do what I'm told. I don't always do the right thing and so my curiosity and promiscuity got the best of me. I started looking at this scene from a whole different point of view trying to figure out how to work it to my advantage.

Within a relatively short time I had gone from a relative nobody to someone who had connections to everything seedy in the neighborhood. I knew all of the prostitutes; I knew all of the crack heads; I knew all of the drug dealers. I knew all of the people who were cheating on their partners, and what time they came in. I learned where the drug spots were because I started to call taxis for young ladies who went to the same addresses. I started to know where certain young ladies would be or where they worked. I learned their schedules.

A happily married man would probably not go out and spend up to four hundred dollars to be with a prostitute. He wouldn't think to take that money out of his household. He might occasionally go to a bachelor party and shell out forty dollars because he feels that's what he needs to do because all the other guys are doing the same thing. Now, introduce crack cocaine to the equation you have a different story.

Crack encouraged behaviors that were unbelievable. I've seen groups of men come into the hotel with one young lady and have an orgy. Unfortunately, I was a witness to a train being run on a woman who had to be in her thirties, but because she was addicted to crack cocaine she allowed young men to take turns having their way with her. All of it seemed normal to me so, what does that say about what was going on with me? I actually found humor in this debauchery. As the manager of the hotel, instead of putting a stop to it I'm cheering the guys on.

Take a woman who became addicted the first time she smoked crack and is, now, two or three months into being an addict she needs money constantly to supply her addiction and she uses her body to get the funds. There's the door opener. I saw women who would reduce themselves to such negative and degrading levels for five or ten dollars. They would allow a man to do things that he's only seen in movies that he would never do with his girlfriend or wife.

Here I was, in a relationship. For all intents and purposes, I should have been faithful—something I didn't know how to be. Instead, I was like a kid in a candy store. Women were always available for sex. Walking in and out like a revolving door. On occasion, I would have to wait until business slowed down so I could step away from the front desk. Sometimes I would have ten to twenty minutes to visit one of the young ladies that frequented the motel. There were times that I would have the security guard watch the desk or just leave it unattended. I always had to gauge it by how the evening was going.

My friends would come by the motel to keep me company and also partake in some of the sexual escapades that went on there. In no way am I trying to put my friends under the bus, but I did need help in getting away with a lot of the things I did. A lot of males call it a bond, where they'll basically say nothing as they watch another friend do some things that are really filthy.

Sometimes my friends joined in, sometimes they didn't. I had my partners in crime. My friends and friends of friends would come by because people knew I pretty much could do what I wanted. They even used the motel rooms themselves. So, I did what a lot of brothers do. I put friends in positions where they could work and have some fun too.

Besides the drug dealers and the prostitutes, on many occasions, I had to deal with a lot of violence. One night, someone set a room on fire as a joke, and I had to rush everyone out in the cold. On another occasion a car was left in the motel's parking lot with bodies in it. Nothing scared me more, though, than the night my life almost came to an end.

I was working the overnight shift on Halloween. I was reading at the front desk which was inside a booth with bulletproof glass. The booth was about fourteen by ten feet with a metal sliding security door. In the event of a fire or other emergency, I would only have to slide the security door open. The booth had a bathroom with another door that led out of the booth. Also, the bathroom had a set of stairs that led to the basement. Essentially, there was really no way in from the outside unless I had it unlocked.

When I first started working they told me to always keep the second bathroom door and the metal security door locked so I would be completely safe. Because of my motel adventures I would leave the door unlocked and go in and out as I pleased. I owned a gun at that time, but didn't have it with me that Halloween night. Three masked men walked through the door, but since it was Halloween, I didn't immediately think anything was wrong. They looked around at the glass booth. I didn't let on that I was nervous, but at that point I realized I had not locked the other door to the bathroom. One of the masked men went around to the security door of the booth and shook the handle. At this point I stood up from my chair, left the book sitting on the desk and remembered the door in the bathroom that led to outside of the booth was unlocked. That door led to a hallway. Instantly, I took off and I ran through the booth, through the bathroom to get the unlocked door.

The three men ran around the booth in the same direction. When they reached the door one of them kicked it open. I caught it just as it flew open and pushed my shoulder on it. The three men yelled out, cursing for me to get away from the door. One of the young men yelled at me, "Big man, get away from the door or I'm going to murder you." At first, I wasn't going to say anything, but being a New Yorker and like many New Yorkers, we don't know how to keep our mouths closed, I decided to yell back as if my words were going to stop anything they might have had behind the door.

The next thing I heard was a gunshot coming through the door. It was the first time I had ever been in close proximity to a gun being fired. I have to admit for a brief second, I was terrified, but what took over me, other than terror, was the thought that I would be murdered if I didn't lock the door. So, as I pushed my left shoulder and my left knee against the door, they fired the one shot—maybe four inches from my shoulder, in fact. The second shot came lower down near between my knees. They didn't realize I wasn't directly behind the door, but actually off to the side. After the second shot I was able to close the door and slide the thick black metal bolt into position. Until this day, I know being a big guy helped save my life because if I was a smaller guy they would have just pushed their way in and killed me.

I ran down the stairs to the basement. I called security on the two-way radio telling them to lock themselves in a room. Unfortunately, our guard was unarmed and there wasn't going to be much he could do. As I was warning the security guard I heard seven more shots. I knew they were using a high-caliber weapon because the door was made of very thin metal and the bullets were tearing through it like paper. About ten to fifteen minutes later the security guard told me I could come upstairs. I saw the door was riddled with holes. I believe they thought I may have still been holding the door so they shot high and low with all intent to kill me. One of the bullets came through the metal door and left a large hole in the floor. Another bullet went through the door into a lead pipe, dented it, and ricocheted into a stone wall. Another bullet went into the gooseneck of a sink which a police officer later told me was made of solid steel.

Most people in my position would have quit the job the next day and not come back. However, not only did I come back, I was still floating around the hotel as if nothing had happened because I wasn't about to let a small thing like being shot at interrupt my business at the hotel. You hear people say all the time the Lord was with them. Some just say it because it sounds good. They got lucky at some things they did and they like to attach the Lord's name to it. I don't understand it, but the Lord wrapped his hands around me for some strange reason because that night being shot at should have ended it all.

Most people who are suffering from dysfunction don't want to admit the depths they've sunk to when connected to sex. They act appalled that someone would be in opposition to their behavior. We try to come up with excuses about exploration. Present men with opportunities where they can't get caught and even some of the greatest men will stoop to the lowest.

We see it on television, we see it in magazines, and movies and we ask that question, "Why would a man who seems to have so much risk it all for sex?" Elliot Spitzer, a married New York governor threw away his career and his marriage. Tiger Woods admitted to having sexual relations with multiple women outside of his marriage. He was out of control and had a sexual addiction.

Take a look at history and you will see there have always been men who threw everything away for sex. Why? The answer is easy; you don't walk by a vault of money that's not being guarded. If you had an opportunity to walk into a bank, pick up the money, walk out, spend the money come back the next day- without any serious penalty, and the vault is still open, why would you stop?

I know as you're reading you're thinking, didn't he think about his health? What about AIDS? What about more people trying to rob the motel? When you're living the life I lived you do think about it, you consider it, you try to take the necessary precautions—condoms and whatever, but you're still going to do what it is you feel you want to do.

This chapter was difficult for me to write because to admit it to the world means that I have to look back into myself and consider what I allowed myself to be and know that I was completely out of control. It's not easy. Before I knew the Lord would actually love someone like me, I didn't know how to love myself completely. I thought I knew love. I thought I had found love a few times up until this point in my life, but I didn't know how to love me. I didn't know how to allow myself to love myself through my mistakes, through the changes, through my failures. I always hid from Him. I always found an excuse. I always found a way to be comical through my pain. I found a way to make any situation, no matter how disgusting, have a little more positive spin to it. I didn't know the Lord had planted the seeds of a writer or an author in who I was. I just knew I wanted sex and I was in the perfect environment to have it.

My first marriage was in the early nineties, and it's a shame I can't remember the date, but that's how bad my marriage was. When I was just coming to my end run at the motel I was still out doing God knows what. There were no limits. There was no floor and there was no ceiling. If I had the opportunity I took it.

For example, one of the housekeeper's daughters used to come and spend time at the hotel while her mother cleaned rooms. This young lady had a baby of about a year old. I thought she was about eighteen or nineteen. On a Sunday when I was filling in for someone, I finagled my way into getting close to this young lady.

We decided to go back to my house because we didn't want the other housekeepers to know what was going on. Once we were at my house she asked me, "I thought you didn't like young girls." I'm thinking to myself, what did she mean? "I know you're young. You're not the type of young lady I normally chase, but you fit."

She was thick and available and that was all that I needed at the time. We are about to get into it and she tells me she's seventeen-years-old. I thought about it for only a split moment and then realized I didn't even care. To make it worse, she had to bring her baby because she didn't have a babysitter. So here we are getting into it and her child is lying on the bed. I'm trying to have sex with her while he's sleeping. Attempting to be cautious not to bounce the bed too much, and at the same time keep him from rolling off the bed.

Finally, I became frustrated and decided to put a pallet of pillows and blankets on the floor and put the baby on it. Once the baby was out of the way I got back to business. How deviant and how sick my behavior was? I asked myself would I want something like that done to my daughter. Would I want my sons to do that to someone else's daughter?

When I look at the positions I placed myself in I would bet money, with all I had done in the three and a half years working at the motel, I had to be in close proximity to the AIDS virus. So, why did I continue? Why did I take those chances? Why did I take those chances? Because when you want power and control and you convince yourself of that want, when that want becomes so addictive that it actually has a taste, you block out the extreme negatives. You don't consider the consequences. It's almost, whatever. You focus on the immediate. Also, when you can't love yourself, a part of you is secretly routing for you to die. Your death would end all the pain within yourself. That's the side that most guard heavily. They don't want others to see their weaknesses and pain. If others are let in, then they might not see the successful individual they have made people believe they are. So people hide it with alcohol. Some people hide it with doing drugs. Some people hide it with a combination of both. Some people hide it with frequent dating so that not one person gets a true idea of the individual.

    Not all of my motel experiences have been negative. I remember a crack head named Evelyn, who went by the name of Lou, lived in my apartment building in Rochdale Village. She was a statuesque five foot eleven inches tall. When she wore heels she was extra gorgeous. When she first moved into the neighborhood men were all over her, ogling and wanting to get next to her. Every neighborhood has that one sexy woman that people love to see walk by and dream of getting with. Evelyn was that woman. However, not too long after moving in rumors started going around that she was using crack. The maintenance men in the building said that they just had to talk to her and they could do something with her if they had the money. I found out firsthand the rumors were true. I had my opportunity with her in the staircase of my building. Like I mentioned before when an addict realizes that you are a resource they will make occasional appearances. She came to the house a couple of times for "a date" and I finally had to tell her to stop coming because my grandmother was starting to wonder why this older lady was coming to see this young man. Evelyn was eventually evicted and it wasn't until about four years later when I was working at the motel that I would see her again.

    She came into the hotel still looking pretty good, but you could see the wear and tear of drug use on her face. We reconnected and off and on she would come in at different times with different men that she was prostituting with. She'd come down to the front desk and I would talk to her. Sometimes I put her in another room and we'd do what we do and she'd go on about her business because she made her ten or fifteen dollars. I remember her coming in one night, though, looking horrible. She had lost so much weight I almost didn't recognize her. She didn't look healthy. Her skin did not look good. She was no longer the attractive women I met as a teenager. She almost looked like a monster. She had an odor the way a homeless person smells when they haven't washed for a while.

In New York, we called them crack fiends because they just looked like shells of themselves. She came into the motel because she wanted to get into something. I told her no. I didn't want to have anything to do with her. She said to me, "Keith, I really need a room to lay my head down." I thought no, because if I let her lay down in a room, I wouldn't have been able to get her out when my replacement came in and I was going to have a problem. "No, Lou, I can't let you have a room." She begged and begged then she left. She came back about five minutes later. "Please, I have nowhere to go."

Even amongst all the evil that I had done, in my heart, I still had a soft place for people in need. I shook my head, and I remember telling her, "You know I'm going to get in a lot of trouble messing with you. You're going to get me fired, but okay here", and I gave her a key to an outside room in the back of the motel. "You have to be out of the room by six-thirty." It was about four-thirty in the morning, and the next shift was coming in at eight. By telling her to leave by 6:30 that gave me time extra time to work with. Evelyn went toward the back rooms and I went back to work.

I totally lost track of the time and before I knew it it was a quarter to seven. All I thought was how I was going to get this crack head out of the room and not lose my job. When I went to the room I was angry to see the door was open because I would always tell anyone I gave an outside room to not leave the doors open. I didn't want homeless people or worse, crack heads, coming into the room stealing things. I walked in and the room was perfectly clean. Not used, not touched in any way as if no one had ever been in it. The key was lying in the middle of the bed. I didn't think twice about it. I picked the key up, looked around the room to make sure everything was in order, closed the door, and left everything in good condition for the next shift.

It wasn't until 1993 that I learned what happened to Evelyn and the motel room. I was walking around Green Acres Mall with my first wife, my son, and mother-in-law. I was lagging behind unenthusiastically when I happened to see a nicely shaped rear-end. I wanted to get a better look at it. I told my wife and mother-in-law, "Go ahead, I'll catch up. I want to check something out over here." I made sure they walked far enough ahead and I doubled back to look at, what I thought was, the most perfectly ample backside. As I'm getting closer I see short hair and a beautiful cocoa complexion on an Amazon.

Of course, now, I wanted to see what she looked like. When the woman turned around I stopped dead in my tracks. My mouth dropped open and I was in shock. It was Evelyn. I couldn't believe what I saw. At the same time Evelyn looked up to see me staring at her. She dropped everything and ran over to me like an Olympic athlete and pretty much tackled me. With that full body of hers she almost knocked me over. She squeezed me and gave me the biggest kiss as if we were dating. The biggest tears started to trickle down her face and she said to me, "You saved my life."

"I saved your life?" In my mind I had contributed to the very thing that was destroying her. I was helping her prostitute in the motel so she could feed her drug habit. Every once in a while I'd give her a little pocket change so I could have my turn at her before she was at her worst. So I was dumbfounded that she would say that I saved her life. She stepped back and wiped her tears.

"Do you remember that night that I asked you to give me the room?"

"Yes."

"Do you remember how many times you told me no?"

"I told you no quite a few times."

"Well, I was walking out the front of the motel, dejected because you had told me no. I took a deep breath and I came back in and I asked you one more time to please give me somewhere to lay my head and you changed your mind and said yes. Well, you saved my life that night."

I still didn't understand what she meant.

"When you gave me the key, there was no way for you to know, but I had been raped." She said, "Earlier that evening, a John that I picked up had beaten me and raped me and pretty much had his way with me and I had nowhere to go. I had been walking around all evening, hurting, bleeding and you were the only person I could think of because of how nice you treated me when we did what we did. No matter how many times we had been together you always treated me with respect and I always knew you weren't an ordinary person even though you were paying for sex. When I got to the room, I had the key in my hand. What I thought about was you saying if I don't get up, you were going to lose your job."

Now, in my mind I remember because I was scared to death that if I didn't get her out of that room, there was no way I was going to be able to explain to the next shift guy how this young lady got into a room that wasn't rented. So, now, I'm looking at her and I'm blown away.

She continues, "At that moment I thought, if I lay down, I won't wake up. I will not be able to get up in the time that you gave me. I took myself that night straight to the rehab center."

JCAP was a well know drug rehabilitation center in the neighborhood.

"I realized that if you lost your job, you wouldn't be there to help other women like me. After my time in JCAP, I got myself together. I got my addiction under control, I have since, as you can see, gained my weight back. I have gotten my daughter back. I have a job and I have a house and I owe it to you because you gave me an opportunity to rest my head even if it meant your job."

I stood listening to Evelyn as if she wasn't talking about me. She was gorgeous again, even more so than when she first moved into my building. She held my arm as if I was a long lost friend, but I was just one of her Johns that treated her better than the rest. I didn't think I was any better than the others. No, I didn't beat, rape, or verbally abuse her, but I robbed her of her humanity for a long time even before I saved her life as she says. I was completely humbled by Evelyn's gratitude.

There are roads in our lives that help shape who we become. It all depends on the choices we make. The question is what roads will you take to outline the foundation for the rest of your life? I know there are other men who are lost like I was. They don't know how to make conscious decisions on how to be the type of man they want to be. I don't have regrets about how I lived my life. I have regrets about not being able to see a better me, sooner. I understand, however, in order for me to be where I am now I had to endure some tough roads. It is my past that allows me to be able to reach out to others and say 'I've been there, and I know you can do better.'

Hearing the Lords Voice & Finding Love

Once I started to see the world different, it was time to get my life in a better place. That meant I sat down and started being honest about what was keeping me from the happiness and the peace that I so desperately wanted.

I knew while I was getting myself together I had to get home straight. I had to start becoming the man that Tiffany needed me to be. She is someone totally different from anyone else that I have discussed in this book. Before I explain why I have to start from the beginning of how we met. Tiffany and I met in 1995 when she was nineteen years old and I was twenty-eight years old, at York College. I joke that it was my second tour of duty at York because I returned after I was academically dismissed.

I was the assistant coach of the women's basketball team and I remember seeing this incredibly attractive young lady come into the gymnasium to watch her friends play basketball. From conversations I could tell she was intelligent, but by the way she was dressed, I thought she was poor. Actually, the way I remember it, and as arrogant as I was at that time, I told my friends "You know if you clean her up, she'll actually look pretty good."

Tiffany was really quiet and stayed to herself most of the time while she was in the gym. I asked her out. Until this day she swears my technique was see-through and she knew I was going to ask her out, but hey it worked. I struck up a conversation about gender inequality when dating.

"How come men have to pay for everything when they ask a woman on a date?" I asked.

"I don't think they should have to," she replied.

"I mean, if I use my car to come get you, drive you to the movie theatre, and pay for the tickets I think the least my date could do is buy the popcorn and soda."

"I would not have a problem paying for snacks if we went on a date."

"Really, so do you want to go see a movie?"

"Sure, why not?"

A few days later while driving to the movie theatre I got the opportunity to ask Tiffany about the way she dressed. How uncouth and arrogant I was.

"You know you are really pretty. How come you don't dress better?"

"The reason why you don't see me in a bunch of name brand clothes is because I own a house. The money people spend trying to impress others I use to keep a roof over my head."

Let's be honest about something. You're going to be a little skeptical when a nineteen-year-old tells you they own a house, but looks like she walked out of a homeless shelter. So, no I didn't believe her and figured if she was lying it didn't make a difference. I figured Tiffany was going to be another trophy on the shelf of my ego boost—or so I thought.

I was truthful with her about my marital status at the end of our date. That's when the candy store was closed. I was like a little kid looking through the window at everything I couldn't have. I think I went through every line, every trick, everything I had in my game book to get her to look past the fact that I was married. Everything that I used to get over on other women wasn't even making a dent past Tiffany's defenses. She actually told me, "I have two jobs and a house. I am too cute and have too many men that want to get with me to lower myself to be any man's mistress. There is nothing you can do for me that I can't do for myself or find someone that isn't married to do for me."

I had met my match in self-confidence. She was a young well-put-together woman that was going to play second to no one. She had set the ground rules. We could be friends, but if I wanted more then I would need to find it with someone else. She wasn't going to be a pawn in my game. That only fueled my fascination with her. It's true when they say the more you can't have something the more you want it. I remember we danced together at a school function and I was just so into her that I told one of my friends, "Someday, she's going to be mine. That's my little diamond in the rough right there. I'm telling you." There's no way for me to know that what was coming out of my mouth at that time, was my future. Tiffany left school a couple of weeks after the dance. She never said she was leaving. I would ask her friends about her and all they would say was she was okay.

Five years later, I was separated from my wife and living with my parents, again. I had just left the athletic track because I was working out that evening. I sat in my car and I remember saying, "Lord if you could just send me someone who understands me." I didn't think I was worthy of love at that time so I just asked for someone to understand me. I drove near my house and stopped into the grocery store on the boulevard. As I was about to get back in my car I happened to see this gorgeous young lady in a sharp business suit and heels getting off the bus. I immediately went into pimp mode.

"Why are you looking so mean?" She barely looked at me, rolled her eyes, and kept walking. "Hey, I know you," I yelled to her.

Without missing a step she turned towards my direction with an attitude like 'Who is this saying he knows *me*?' The frown turned into a smile when she recognized me. She walked over to the car and gave me a hug. We weren't into the conversation more than a couple of minutes when Tiffany asked, "Are you still married?" Well, technically I was so what do I say? I looked her right in the face and said, "Let me be honest. Yes, I am but I am separated from my wife and I'm back home living with my grandmother and mother."

I offered her a ride home which was only about five blocks away from my house. We sat outside her house—the same house she told me she owned when she was nineteen, but I had never seen—and talked for about an hour. Catching up on what happened over the past five years. She was tired from a long day's work so the only thing left was to see where we could go from there.

"Here's my number and email address," I gave her a piece of paper I scribbled on. "I'm not going to ask you for your number now, but I know you're going to do like the average women, hold onto it for four or five days and then give me a call." She laughed and went into the house. By the time I got home and signed on to the internet I had received email from her that read "I'm not your average woman", with her telephone number attached.

October of 2000 we started dating and I have to admit it is the longest and best relationship I have ever been in, but it did not go without its bumps—okay craters in the road caused by my self-destructive behavior. I continued to go to the Big Girl Parties. I continued to sleep with other women. I still hadn't learned to be monogamous, but I was great at lying and pretending to be.

I learned to keep my personal life and my perverted life very separate. We were well into the third year of our relationship before I was busted for the first time. It was not a pleasurable experience. It was actually the worst feeling of any relationship I had ever been caught cheating in. I went to bed late one night and left my email open and Tiff opened it by accident. I know it sounds crazy, but before that she wasn't into snooping and going through my things. Tiff found an email, from a young lady I had been with, that was very detailed about our very non-platonic relationship. Unknown to me she came to bed and didn't go back to sleep. She was up for the rest of the night until the alarm clock rang.

Tiff initiated our lovemaking that morning and I was all too willing to participate. What man wouldn't want to wake up to a woman ready to give him pleasure? Afterward, getting ready for work, I was singing in the shower. I can't help, but laugh because Tiff always reminds me of that. Once we were both dressed we got into the car because our morning routine consisted of driving into Brooklyn and dropping her off a couple of blocks from my job so she could catch the train.

Well, we were listening to the radio and I was singing along because I was on cloud nine. We came to a stoplight a few blocks away from where she usually got out and Tiff turned the radio down.

"Can I ask you something?" She asked very calmly in her Tiffany way. If anyone knows my wife she has a very calm demeanor. Even when other people seem to be falling apart around her she is able to hold it together to get the job done.

"Sure baby, what's up?" I answered with child-like giddiness.

"How long have you been cheating on me?"

It was like someone had cut the electricity off as the New Year's Eve Ball was dropping. I wasn't sure what to say. I wasn't sure if someone had contacted her or how she knew after all this time. We had almost four years of no drama and now I was being confronted. I honestly was thinking what in the world happened between our lovemaking and getting into the car that I missed.

"Baby, what are you talking about? I'm not cheating on you?"

"Keith, I need you to be honest with me. Please don't insult me by lying."

"Tiff, whoa, I don't know what you're talking about. I'm not cheating on you. Did someone tell you I was cheating?"

By this time I had pulled into our regular stop where she caught the train. I was nervous, sweating, just hoping that she would accept what I was saying and the bad feeling I was having would just go away, but it didn't.

"Who's Kim?" She asked me as calmly as the first question.

"Oh, Kim", I tried to blow it off like that name meant nothing; "Kim is a friend of mine. She likes me, but nothing is going on."

"Really? Kim likes you an awful lot. She likes you so much she can't wait until the next time she sees you."

Tiff is no idiot. At no time, ever, in this relationship had she been that. Now, she had played the fool because of me, but that's because she cared about me not because she lacked intelligence. I want the world to understand that. This is a very incredibly savvy and smart woman. I couldn't see her for who she was because I had been the man I had been my whole life. Tiff and I have since called this our Bill Clinton moment because no matter how much evidence she gave me to show that I had been busted I continued to declare my innocence in any sexual activity with Kim.

"Yeah she does like me a lot, but nothing is going on…".

"She likes you so much that she had to go to the doctor to make sure she's not pregnant. That's a lot of liking wouldn't you say?"

"What, what, I…" I tried to think of what I could say to counte-rattack.

"You know I don't believe you, right?"

All I could think is why is she so calm? Why isn't she screaming and cursing? Who makes love to someone they know they are going to break up with in less than an hour? At that moment I was defeated. I put my head down in shame.

"I know, and you shouldn't."

"Here's what I want you to do," She began to tell me what she wanted as if she was planning a recipe for dinner, "When I come home I don't want you there. I don't want to see you. I want you to go home get all your things, and leave your keys with my mother. Do we have an understanding?"

"Yes."

Tiffany got out of the car and began to walk away. She didn't even slam the door when she left. I immediately started calling her cell phone hoping she would answer as she walked to the train station. She never looked back. She never looked at her phone. She didn't break her stride. I called and called and called as I watched her walk out of sight.

By the time I reached my job I was a ball of emotions. I am normally a very polished professional educator, but I was broken. My eyes were red, tears were falling down my face, and as soon as I walked through the door I met my boss. She grabbed me into her office and asked me what happened. The only words I could get out were, "I f----d up."

I asked my boss if I could take a class period to get myself together and she told me to take two. I must have called Tiff twenty times begging to just get an audience; begging to be heard; begging her to allow me to speak on my behalf about my behavior. Before the end of the day, she did. She gave me an opportunity to discuss what I had done and I took it to come somewhat clean. My belief was if I'm wrong then I'll be wrong, but a cheater is like an addict and you have to hit rock bottom before you give in completely; or else all he is doing is paying lip service.

That's exactly what I was doing. I didn't want to lose Tiffany, but I wasn't ready to change either and so I cried and I pleaded and I became everything that a sorrowful man becomes. She forgave me and took me back. So, like a drug dealer who just had his operation infiltrated, I shut things down for a little while. I wanted to let the heat die down a bit before I set up again.

That was the first time in my life that I had feelings inside me I didn't know how to explain. It was like butterflies times a hundred, but they were piercing at the inside of my stomach instead of tickling. It is the sick feeling that you get when you get a phone call in the middle of the night if you're a parent. It's the same feeling that you get if a Policeman is coming to your door and you know it's going to be bad news. I just had an ill feeling that I had messed this relationship up and it was at that moment that what Tiffany meant to me really started to take hold. You would think a man who has a wonderful woman like I do would have enough inside of him to say I don't want to lose her so let me stop. Let's give this relationship what it deserves. I behaved for a couple of weeks, but then my suppliers, the drug dealers in my life if you want to call them that; the women started calling again.

When you're unhappy and trying to live a dual life the conflict inside you is like a war. The collateral damage that comes from that war is the wives, the girlfriends, fiancées, your children, and your relationship with your friends. You may share with your friends some of the pains that you're going through, but if they're not going to come clean with you and tell you that you need to choose all they're doing is tossing more fuel into the fire.

Another part of the damage is not being able to sleep at night. I started to feel extreme guilt. I didn't feel comfortable many nights climbing in bed next to Tiffany knowing the things I had done. I didn't feel at ease with myself and then the minute that I thought I had something under control, I got an email or I got a text or I got some video or I got a picture. I got something that would drag me right back to the madness.

I remember having an affair on a trip I took to the Bahamas with my friends. I met Judy at the resort we were staying in. She was also from New York. For three straight days Judy and I acted out a Harlequin Romance. Steamy, passionate, and something that should have been completely off limits for someone who was as in love with my girlfriend as I said I was. On Judy's last day at the resort she said to me, "You know you have such energy around you. You have a light that radiates from you. You really should just give in to that."

"What are you talking about?" I was completely clueless.

"I know these past few days were exactly what they were. When we get back to New York I know we aren't going to see each other anymore and I actually don't want us to see each other again."

"What are you talking about? I thought we'd maybe hook-up..."

"No. You have a woman, I have a man and this was fun for what it was, but you have something whatever it is that you need to follow that you need to consider."

All I could think was how do you sleep with somebody for three days and then just cut it off. She left, but I didn't stop thinking about her. The next evening one of the female employees who served us and who teased me about moving in with her in the Bahamas sat down at my table.

"Do you have a couple of minutes?" She asked me.

"Sure."

She smiled and said, "I want to thank you for treating me so nice the six days that you've been here."

"What do you mean?"

"I know you're a big flirt. I know that you're a ladies' man. I saw you with the Spanish lady and I saw you with the different women always joking and laughing, but you were always so kind to me and I know I'm a thick girl and I know you said you like thick girls, but I want to thank you for treating me with respect." She continued, "Sometimes we have people that come here and they treat us workers as if we're less than human, and I want to thank you for treating me like a woman. You made me feel tremendous this week and I wasn't joking. I would love to have you stay here with me, but I know that you have a woman back home."

I'm sitting there thinking. I never told her I had a woman. I never said anything about my personal life. So, where did she get this from? She reached over, took my hand, looked me in the eyes and said, "You have an energy that is just so bright. Don't mess it up by giving it away to people who don't deserve it. I bet you have a wonderful woman at home. Be the man to her that she needs. You're not going to find it in these streets. You're a good man and you're going to be an even better man with a good woman by your side. Be that man to that woman. You can see it all over you."

For the second consecutive night, someone was telling me that they see more in me and that they see the same thing as the other person. I kept that inside and when I came home, realizing that I was being given a sign, I knew it was time to get ready to marry Tiffany and to be the man that I was supposed to be.

When I got home, Tiff and I were joking around. She asked me if I had a good time. I told her I had a wonderful time. Of course, I did not mention the little side romance, but what shocked me was how my dog reacted to me when I came back from the Bahamas. Before I took the trip anytime I picked up our Yorkie he would lick my face. After the trip I picked up the dog and he turned away. I would put him closer to my face and he refused to lick me. He kept turning his head away.

Tiff laughed and said, "Awwww, the baby being stubborn." The dog was always happy to see me before. It gave me hugs, jumped in my face; put his front paws on my leg to be picked up. A couple of days went by. I picked him up again, put my face near his, and he turned his head, but when Tiff picked him up he would immediately lick her face. She would hand him over to me and he'd turn his head again. I became afraid the dog would expose me and Tiff would start to wonder why the dog wouldn't lick me anymore.

Because of the dog, I decided that it was time for Tiff and I to move to the next level. I had talked to her about us getting married and we decided that it was that time. This time, I promised, I was going to make my marriage work the right way. I was going to take all the lessons that I had learned from my past mistakes and I was going to make this marriage hold up and be exactly what my first marriage wasn't.

I will be honest that it wasn't easy to go from being male whore to monogamous. People won't let you forget what you were and it starts to become a struggle. This went on for a while and then I found myself confronted with another part of my past: Clara, My affair with her began while I was still with my first wife.

I should have left her so many times, but the demon in me didn't allow it. She didn't care what I was doing while I was not with her. Clara maintained her position as my mistress during my first marriage, to being single then to dating Tiffany. Eventually like anything else that has such a negative grip, you're going to fall. No matter how good you believe you are with handling your business, I don't care how good a player you think you are, you cannot continue an unhealthy lifestyle and not have it blow up in your face.

The woman that is with you regularly—your girlfriend or your wife—starts to notice that you are not being who you were and if she's intelligent she'll start to keep an eye on you to see how things pan out. Tiffany was good at that. She never revealed her cards until she was sure you were caught. She never let her emotions take her to a point where she was speculating. If she confronted you it was because she had all the proof she needed.

Meanwhile, the mistress, in this case, Clara, got tired of being the other woman. She started asking, "How many nights are you going to come here and lay next to me? How many times are we going to be with each other, but not elevate me to the position I deserve?" Clara pretty much shared everything with me just like in a "regular relationship". She not only knew birthdates, children's names she also knew many other things about me.

Imagine fighting the Civil War in the 1860s and someone shows up with nuclear weapons. The game changed completely. I started to feel the pressure from both sides. Clara was putting pressure on me because she couldn't understand how I bypassed her to put another woman on a pedestal. She felt that it was her rightful place to be there because of all that she had endured to make me happy. Plus, Clara was very savvy on the computer and she started to find things that were out there that contained information about Tiff and me.

Tiff could see my personality was changing and I wasn't being who I was supposed to be. I remember one night Tiff was laying next to me and I received an email from Clara. She was questioning my relationship with Tiffany. How could I go out and do this and basically leave her out in the cold? I didn't even know how to respond to it. I figured if I just turned the computer off and eased myself away from it I was good, but I wasn't. Once I had tied peoples' feelings into my sexual desires, I didn't have the convenience of walking away and ignoring Clara. The game is not played that way. I got busted.

Tiffany found out about Clara. She saw the information; she saw the emails and I was caught for the second time. It wasn't pretty. I went right into my mode of begging and pleading and the stabbing butterflies were back. I did everything to convince Tiff to stay with me. Clara was so disgusted with me because as it all came out, she had put in all this time with me and it was like a slap in the face to actually have to just read on the internet about me having this whole other life with someone else. The life she thought I should have been having with her. My two worlds were falling apart and starting to conflict with each other.

In between all of that is when I had had my epiphany. I started to realize that I needed to get right with the Lord. Having to tell Tiff that I had never been monogamous; that I didn't know what I was out here doing; that I didn't know how I was going to control myself; I didn't know what I was going to be; I didn't know how I could make the moves to make myself better. I was scared.

One of the things that started to help me change my life around was attending Bible study. By going to Bible study it allowed me to learn more about the Lord and the Christian faith and what my responsibilities were as a man of God. I started to reconnect with my Christian roots. In seeing my efforts, Tiff opened up to her Christianity. Something she knew about as a child, but never fully enveloped. We started going to church regularly. Reading the Bible and discussing scriptures and how they applied to our lives. Tiffany, eventually, made the choice to be baptized for the first time. This was a very important moment in our lives for both of us, and I didn't know how much at the time.

Tiff being baptized was God's way of putting into place a failsafe for our relationship because He already knew the monster that I was and that I was not going to be able to heal me, alone. So through Tiff connecting to Him, He was going to work His way with me through her. I know this may sound strange to all my non-Christians, but stay with me because this is not about church right now. This is about how God works through someone else to help you. Whether you believe it or not, that's fine, but this is not debate on whether God is real. He is real to *me* so I'm sorry if you just shake your heads and say it's not believable. This is what it is.

Tiff began reading her Bible more often and we began to grow closer as a couple. The two parts at war within me was slowly coming to peace. I now had a new ally in the war. God was that force. He was building the foundation for a renewed me, but the evil habits that shaped me for so long was not going out without a fight.

Women whom I was sexually connected to began to appear on the internet, through the big girl parties and I continued to take chances all over the place. I was risking my life having sex with women that I should not have been with. I was taking chances meaning that I was not protecting myself like I should have and I was risking my life, Tiffany's life, and at no time did I just stop. I just kept telling myself, 'I'm going to leave this alone; I can stop this at anytime." This is the prototypical addict's creed that never works.

I thought being present at the birth of two of my sons was the greatest thing to have happened to me, but it pales in comparison to the day I actually heard God speak. I know you're sitting there thinking: 'Okay, he might have a screw loose. He actually heard God speak?' Yes, I did.

You see, no matter how much you try to hide it your unhappiness sits just under the surface. Many people have learned how to ignore their unhappiness. Some need assistance so they chose alcohol, drugs sex, poor behavior, disrespect of themselves and others or, whatever they can to keep the attention off the real person they are. There are two beings you can't hide the real you from. That's yourself and God, but you can act as if God doesn't exist which many do. I was no different. I knew of God. I knew of the Christian faith. I know of a lot of things, but I never committed to it because it just didn't seem like something that I was going to be a part of.

I was, like many folks, I would say I believe in God, but I'm not religious. I would have different excuses of why I didn't like church and all of them had to do with selfish reasons and like many folks I just didn't want to sit there and hear about something that I just wasn't connected to. I knew God existed, I knew I didn't want to disrespect certain things the church stood for, but to me, the church was God and so my attitude towards the church, reflected my attitude towards God.

The very last time that I got caught, Tiff didn't know she caught me, but she did. A young lady I was dating sent a text to me that she was coming to New York. In her message Vera said she got a hotel room with two beds because after our sexual rendezvous we would need a dry bed to sleep in. Tiff woke me up in the middle of the night. She's very savvy as I said. So she wanted to catch me when I was least likely to try to think fast.

"Who is this person?" She asked me as she was shoving my cell phone into my face. "And why would they say that?"

I tried to sprint through the different lies that I could tell, and she is right in my face so I had to think quickly. "It's a friend of mine. She comes into town and she always texts me little jokes and foolishness like that. You can give her a call and she'll tell you nothing is going on."

Now you might be sitting here saying, how is that a way out? He just completely busted himself. No. A real good male whore has been doing his job so well that he already knows which women will play her position correctly. I knew this woman was not going to throw me under the bus when that phone call was made. When I pressed my cell phone and pressed her number, Tiff was staring at me like a parent who is waiting to hear the lie. I quickly said, "Sweetheart..." and before I could say anything else, Tiff snatched the phone out of my hand.

"Why are you texting my man about getting a hotel room?"

I'm sitting there looking very calm, but inside I am nervous because I know the wrong word and I am out on the street. I could tell Vera was explaining her message to me. The next thing Tiffany said was, "Yeah, you come to New York to go shopping?" She looked up at me while still holding the phone to her ear, "Check this out Keith, I don't know if you think I'm stupid, but I'm not one of these insecure heifers sitting at the bar doggy-posing waiting for some n---a to come give me some attention."

Tiff hung up the phone and threw it at me. She threatened that if I touched her she would break my jaw. This was the first time that Tiffany was really out of character. Anger consumed her and I will be honest I wanted to comfort her, but was afraid she just might break my jaw, as mad as she was, if I touched her. Tiff didn't know that she had me dead to rights. She felt it, but the scenario did not play out the way that she thought so there was no way for her to completely flip on me that evening so she had to ease back, but I realized I now had the advantage. I have to push forward and push forward is what I did.

Of course I thought taking the defense would work so I went at her about checking my phone. I screamed at her about not trusting me and how can I ever change what I was if you're going to keep putting pressure on me. Like any good addict, I have to turn this around at the person who wants me to change. By the time I was done, I had Tiff on the phone calling Vera back and apologizing. It was just stupid. Instead of just giving in, I was going to try to hold on to both sides.

I remember walking into our living room and thinking how long was I going to play this game? How long can I live like this before I get AIDS? I was destroying Tiffany's thoughts about me in every aspect. She was fed up. That night she asked me to leave. I'm thinking to myself, what did I do? I hadn't done anything. I started thinking maybe I should go. She didn't trust me; this was not going to work, but then something inside, the goodness that had been growing, yelled out, 'Don't walk out the door.' This relationship is worth saving. I didn't know how to turn it around. I didn't want to end my relationship and I knew deep down Tiff didn't want me to leave. So I went to her as she sat on the edge of our bed. I got on my knees in front of her with tears in my eyes, and said, "I don't want to leave. Please don't make me leave. I will sleep on the couch if I have to until you take me back into our bed, but please I don't want to lose you."

Her response nearly broke my heart. "Keith, I can't do this anymore. I just can't." Then she said something to me that I've never had a woman say to me in my life. She said, "Listen, it is either God and me or the hoes in the street. It can't be both. Now you're going to have to make a choice."

I couldn't believe she wanted me to make a decision on being a whore or being her boyfriend right there, right at that moment?

The look in her eyes was no longer anger. It was empathy and sorrow. She leaned over and put her hands on mine then said, "You've got to share with me everything that's going on inside of you if I'm to help you."

The tides started to turn. God was taking his position in my life and He was winning the war. He was giving me another ally in Tiffany. We had been together five years by this point and I knew that I was in love, but I had no idea, what it meant to have someone in your corner that was willing to help protect you even if it's from yourself. She continued to break down those walls, "I need to know the evils that you deal with so I can help you."

"Baby, you don't want that." I started to think about all the things I had done to her and to others. Is she serious? She couldn't handle that.

"Yes, I do because if you tell me, then I can protect you when you can't protect yourself."

I was blown away. She wanted me to let her into something that I have been struggling and battling with my whole life. She was strong about it and I knew it was because of the new strength that she got from being baptized. I knew it was her connection to God that allowed her to say those things and it brought a wave of emotions that I had never felt before. It was as if my two allies brought weapons to the battle that I had never seen and they set those weapons off on the enemy and the enemy had no response.

When that wave came over me, it was as if I understood exactly what I needed to do if I was going to become something different. I had to let go of the man that I was and think differently. Feel differently. And so I decided to do exactly that. I decided to give in and say to my woman, "I am going to become what you need me to become. I am going to become the different man, but I need your help."

"That's all I ever wanted," she told me.

That night in my girlfriend's arms, I found peace. I remember going to bed that night feeling different. When I got up that morning, I remember praying first, thanking the Lord for allowing me to still be here after all the foolishness I had done and I remember saying, it's time now. It's time to leave all the foolishness alone. Leave the big girl parties alone. Leave the running around alone. I kept trying to convince myself that I needed to get it together. I needed to be a better man to Tiffany. I needed to be a better person to myself, but habits are hard to break.

I had one last battle to fight. I came up with an excuse for going to New Jersey for a weekend. Tiffany was very trusting, and I abused her trust. She always told me that she didn't have time or energy to follow up on what I was and wasn't doing when I wasn't with her. She said that if she had to spend productive time worrying whether or not a boyfriend was cheating then she couldn't concentrate on the important things in life. I often wondered where she got this wisdom at such a young age. Instead of me respecting the fact that she was giving me the option to do the right thing just because I should I made arrangements to spend the weekend with Kim. Yes, the first mistress Tiffany caught me with. As I was driving two hundred plus miles to the southern part of New Jersey I called Kim.

"Hey, sexy, I'm on my way. I should be there in a little bit."

"Fine, I can't wait to see you."

Everything was working perfectly. My plan was unfolding without any hiccups. I am right where I need to be. I get to the hotel in New Jersey and I give Kim another call to let her know I was there. She said she was on her way and she would be there in fifteen minutes. You may be reading this and thinking, ok so what happened to me promising Tiffany I would be faithful and planning to get married. Well, I still wanted to marry Tiffany and I wanted to be faithful because I did believe that's what she deserved. After all, I loved her with all of my heart, but I was still in that fight. However, I had no idea what was in store for me on this evening that I decided to be unfaithful, yet again. You often hear people say God works in mysterious ways well it doesn't get any better than this.

As I was waiting in the hotel room I got a call from Kim. She told me she was running late because she was having stomach pain.

"I'm going to take something and I'll be on my way."

"Fine, take your time. I'm here for the evening," I told her, "We're good. We have the whole night. Don't worry about it."

So I'm getting the room ready. I put the condoms on the nightstand; I'm watching television, relaxing. A little while later Kim called back. She told me her stomach got worse and she wasn't going to be able to make it. I was too through. I couldn't believe after wasting one of the best excuses to get out of the house then driving all this way I was sitting in a hotel room by myself because she had a stomach ache. I grew angry.

"What do you mean you can't make it? Come on I'm down here. I'm waiting on you. I came a long way to see you."

"I'm sorry. I don't know why my stomach is hurting like this, but I just can't make it. I'm sorry" She hung up the phone.

I slammed the phone down. I started going through my address book to see what replacement was in the area that I could invite over. No one I called picked up. I was stuck for the night. I had traveled two hundred plus miles away from my girlfriend to basically be in an empty hotel room. You couldn't be any more upset than I was.

As I sat there, alone, I thought of all kinds of awful names to call Kim. After all it was her fault that I was there. Consumed in my anger and frustration I didn't realize the tele-ministry playing in the background. I looked at the television and thought I don't need this right now, but I didn't change the channel. I just let it play. Now, let me say I wasn't a big fan of television preaching. I didn't think you could solve the problems of the world in a half an hour. I know, now, the Lord can speak to you at any time, through anybody if you're willing to listen. Two hours passed and four separate pastors gave their message. My anger began to go away and started to be replaced with confusion.

I couldn't wrap my mind around it, but each pastor spoke volumes about something I was dealing with, in my life, at the time. TD Jakes was the fifth and final Pastor to come on. Jakes has a very strong and thunderous presence. He commands your attention even when you may not want to watch. He began to tell the story about a thirty-eight-year-old man with no legs. As he told his story Jakes went into dancing on the stage. He said the man heard that Jesus was coming and instead of making a move, he sat right where he was, angry. So when Jesus came and left the man grew bitter. The people around asked the man, "Why are you so bitter?" He said, "I have no legs and the Messiah came and I missed him." The people replied, "But you knew for days, you knew for weeks that he was coming. You knew that he was coming to the well. Why didn't you simply just roll yourself there? Why didn't you crawl? Why didn't you do something that was going to put you in position to be at that well if you really wanted to see him? And now that he's gone, you're angry and you're frustrated. Well, it's your fault."

At that point Jakes turned to the camera, and it zoomed in on his face. He said, "I don't know who this message is for but I'm talking to somebody out there who's thirty-eight-years-old, who needs to understand that God is speaking to you right now." I thought I was going crazy. Is God speaking to me?

My grandmother once told me you don't shy away from speaking about God to others who don't know him because when it's time, the Lord will let you know exactly who He is and then all those times that you heard of His glory will come to the forefront and you'll understand. I was starting to understand and it was scaring me to death. I got down on my knees and the tears began to fall. Through the tears, I started hearing the voice of my great grandmother. I remember how she wouldn't go to sleep without hearing the Bible read to her. I remember she would get up in the morning and thank the Lord for waking up and then read the Bible. She lived to ninety-five years old. I had the blessing of living with her for a year when I learned more about life in that short time than in any textbook. I understood why she was the matriarch of my family. Then it started to make sense.

My grandmother, her daughter, never did anything without putting God into it. If I or anyone else was going through a trying time she always asks, "Did you pray about it?" So here I was on my knees, tears streaming down my face and I'm praying. I'm praying hard and loud. I'm praying out loud. What am I doing? I'm an educator. I'm a father. I have so many things that are positive. What am I doing to myself? What have I done to myself? I was so emotional. I did something I've never done in my life. I looked up to the ceiling as if it wasn't there as if I was staring straight up into the heavens and I said, "Ok, Father. You got me. I'm broken. What do I do now? I'm unhappy. What is it that you want from me?" Now I was willing to say, "God, you step in. Why is it you kept me alive? What is it that I'm supposed to be?"

Now, once I humbled, it wasn't like television and you see sparks and magic and bright lights and anything like that. No bright lights, the television was still playing in the background, but I felt as if a weight had been lifted. That I allowed myself to give into my own pain and ask God to help me. I felt as if I didn't need anyone or anything else. It was always about me. It was always about my sexual urges. It was always about the things that I wanted. It was always about the things that made me who I was. When I got up from the floor, I wiped my face. I sat back quietly and I meditated. One of the first things that came to mind was to call my grandmother. I woke her up, but she could tell something was wrong. I don't care what time of night it is, if you call her, she's going to talk to you. I said, "Gramps? I think I heard the Lord's voice. What do I do?"

"It's about time," she responded, "What you do is whatever He told you to do."

"What if he didn't tell me anything?"

"Well, sit still and wait and he'll tell you."

"Yes ma'am. I'll give you a call in the morning when I'm getting ready to head back to NY."

"No problem. You give me a call and make sure you say your prayers tonight."

"Okay."

I needed someone else to talk to. I was having anxiety at this newfound spirit. As I sat there trying to figure out who else I could call that would reaffirm what I was feeling the phone rang.

Now, what I am about to say is very important. I want you to make a note of it. In the Christian faith I believe people give the devil way more credit than he deserves. They never stop and think about their role in the things that they do. The devil can't make you do anything. He can make suggestions and often will put things in place in an attempt to make you stray from your God-given path.

When I picked up the phone my ex-wife was on the other end. By this point we had been apart for six years. I don't remember why she called, but our conversations were hardly ever pleasant. Once she was done with the purpose of her call I asked her, "Can I speak to you a second?" She said, "Sure."

"I want to come clean about something."

"Ok."

I hesitated and realized I was about to do something I have never done before. I was going to come clean about the awful husband I was to her. I confessed that when we were married I cheated on her and that I was out doing all the things that people thought I was doing. I wasn't expecting her to be elated, but I didn't think she was going to explode like she did. I received a tirade of how I was exactly what everyone had said I was. She was foolish for not seeing it and she couldn't believe it. She didn't care.

"What is this? Some type of twelve step program. Because if it is I don't care. I'm never going to forgive you."

"I'm not asking you for forgiveness," I said, "I'm just telling you the truth to put it out there so that you know what happened."

"I don't care no matter what you do; nothing will come good to you until you do right by me!" She slammed the phone down.

She couldn't be any more wrong. You see, man can't say how another person is forgiven. Only God can forgive you that way and when he does you don't have to worry about how man feels. When I got off the phone, I felt a lot better. I felt like I was slowly peeling off the layers of dead weight. Before falling asleep from exhaustion I said my prayers.

When I woke up the following morning the first thing I did was pray. Then I called a colleague and friend that I knew would be beneficial on my new Christian walk. Bostic and I worked together for a few years. He made no hesitation of letting people know where his faith was and he was very easy to talk to.

"Brother, listen. I think I heard the Lord's voice last night, but I'm not sure what I'm supposed to do I just know I want to be something and do something different today."

"Amen, Brother," he was excited to hear my good news, "Here's what you need to do—"

Brother Bostic told me I needed to start going to Bible study so I could truly get an understanding of what the Bible is and what it means so I would be able to have some type of guidance in my life. He also suggested at least once a week have a Godly conversation with someone who's in the faith that way I could start getting comfortable with learning how to talk to others who are believers who can also help me strengthen the spiritual walk I was undertaking. The third thing he said was to find a good faith-based church, but to take my time and allow my spirit to help guide me.

All three of these seemed like strange requests to me. I had never thought about Bible study. I think the last time I was there I was about seven and my mother forced us to go to Sunday school. The thought of having a Christian conversation with somebody once a week was like speaking a foreign language. I was the biggest sinner that ever lived so how was I going to do that and go to church on a regular, not happening. However, I listened and I was open to the suggestions.

After my conversation with Bostic I checked out of the hotel. I didn't bother calling Kim back. I made the decision right there that was a dead issue. My goal was to go home and continue my transformation I had to call my grandmother again.

My grandmother told me she had been praying for this change in me for the longest and she always knew I would get to this point. My grandmother helped me get ready for the call I was dreading. For the first time I had to be honest with Tiffany about what I had been our entire relationship to that point.

Hearing Tiffany's voice that morning was if I was hearing it for the first time. Everything, I mean everything was so different. I didn't know how I was going to tell her the truth. I made up an excuse to get off the phone. I told her I had to concentrate on the road. I wasn't ready yet.

As I continued to drive I started to replay my entire life in my head. The other cars around me were a blur. I was begging for an answer. This *has* to be the way out for me. This *has* to be something different because everything else I had done didn't have anything Godly connected to it. I had been keeping journals off and on over the years leading up to that point and in those journals I had been stating that maybe I should turn my life over to a higher power. Maybe I should meditate more. Maybe I should become more spiritual. Maybe I should just do things differently because things just weren't working and here was the culmination of that.

When I finally made it home I knew I couldn't just come through the door blurt out "Hey Honey! I heard from the Lord and I've been cheating on you all of these years." I wanted to ease into this new step that I was taking, but I knew eventually I was going to have to come clean if I was going to do this right. First I had to get myself right. I did exactly as my friend said. I came home and I joined a Bible study group—his. And because he and I had been friends for over eight years at the school where I was teaching, it made it easier to attend a Bible study where he was the instructor because I respected him as an educator and respected him as a man and now I was going to learn that respecting him as a Christian was just going to make our friendship even better.

Bible Study

One of the things that will help a person once they've changed is support as well as learning as much as they can about new things. As they grow into the person that they're becoming, now that they've made these changes in their life, finding something else to focus on helps to remove them from the situations and circumstances that kept them in the frame of mind that they were in.

In my case, I needed Bible study. I wasn't ready to join a church. I wanted to go to church, but I wasn't ready to become an active member of anyone's church. During church the pastor can have a tremendous sermon, but you can't ask any questions. You can't get into a dialogue back and forth about what's being talked about in the sermon. If you don't get it, you may leave that Sunday with a great feeling, but without the resounding message that's needed. In Bible study, you get to discuss what you are hearing and learning.

Two weeks from my epiphany, I showed up to Bostic's church on a Wednesday night for Bible study. I felt comfortable in the smaller setting of the study class. In the past when I attended church I often felt like an outcast amongst all of the regulars. I felt like I wasn't supposed to be there. In contrast the Bible study classes were more intimate and allowed time for individual tutoring. I took a seat to the side. Brother Bostic welcomed me then introduced me to everybody in the group and explained our connection then we went right into the lesson for the evening.

I honestly enjoyed what I heard. I was learning about God. I had been in church in the past; that wasn't anything new, but listening to the feedback that came from the discussions made the word of God stand out in a way unlike it ever stood out before. When you receive bits and pieces of something over the years, it's all just jammed inside your head. The Bible study classes made things so much clearer.

The class was set up just like a college classroom. There was a clear distinction of where the class was going and what the class was about. I have to honestly say it was tremendous to hear what people were saying, what direction people were going in with their conversations and I just sat back and I was thinking I can get into this. At the end of the two hours, I sat down with my partner, Bostic.

"I'm so happy that you made it, Brother. That's a big step because I know when you talked to me a couple of weeks ago how excited you were about what happened," he cautioned me, "Some people will turn around and let that fall to the wayside so I'm glad that you're here."

"Bostic, man, thank you for taking time with me and inviting me here. Thanks for being somebody I could turn to."

"Well, I have some bad news,"

"Here we go," I said ready to be disappointed.

"Well, next week is the last week of Bible study for this class. Then there's a break for a couple of weeks then we get back together."

"Okay," I continued to listen.

"So, for you to start the class from the beginning you have to come back in five weeks."

I took a deep breath and said, "Okay, no problem. I'm going to be here."

When I was driving home I felt overwhelmed. I started out to do something and it didn't work the way I planned. I figured I would get into the class right away and get on my journey. Now there was going to be a delay. One of my first reactions was to quit and go back to what I was comfortable with, but I didn't want to do that. I didn't want to return to being the old me. In my mind and soul, I was content on sticking it out. So in the meantime I started preparing myself. I purchased a study bible: The Life Application Series Study Bible. I talked to my grandmother as much as possible about the scriptures and what she learned from them. Time went by faster than I thought.

When I went to the new Bible study class I was as nervous as the first day that I had become a teacher. I don't know why. I can tell you right now as you're reading this, the things that we allow to get under our skin can be tremendous. Even though it might be a very minute thing, depending on the feelings that we attach to it, it can seem tremendous. I was sitting in the pews of the church very quietly as the instructors were sectioning off the different classes. Those of us who were attending for the first time started out in the "Red Book". The Red book was an introductory to becoming a disciple. The class lasted thirty-four weeks which equivalent to almost three college courses. As you increase your knowledge of the Bible you move on to different colored study guides. I realized that this was serious business. It wasn't just about sitting around talking. I had to read. I had homework assignments. I was almost intimidated.

Bostic is a tremendous friend and more like a brother. He is a great guy. He had been a mentor to me when I first started teaching. So, it made me feel confident to have him as my instructor in Bible study and to have him as my brother in the Word. Some may also call him an accountability Brother or a Brother in the Spirit. He is someone who helps to keep me on track when I can't seem to find the answer. Bostic is someone who has vast knowledge and experience in the Christian faith and so to have him as a mentor in school, working with him and then to have him now as my beginning instructor, made it much more comfortable for me.

At the start of the group, we had about fifteen people. Bostic told me right before class, "What you're going to notice is in the red book is where we have the largest number of people who come to Bible study. By the time we get to the end of the class, that number may drop down to half and if you finish the first book, when you move onto your second book you'll notice the numbers drop down tremendously because people just lose that fire, that determination to want to keep learning." I took it all in.

I was just happy to have those who were in our class there because the discussions that came from the topics were fantastic. I was finally growing and having an extended spiritual family, I felt tremendous. I felt completely changed: like a new man. Each week that I learned something new, I couldn't wait to share it. I couldn't wait to talk to someone about what I read and what we discussed. I remember highlighting so many different things in my Bible to talk to someone about. I remember Bostic and I would talk on the phone almost every night. I'd see him at work and we'd discuss some more. Our Godly conversations were just awesome. My faith became my anchor.

Jesus is the example that we strive to be like. Many people have their own role models and their own picture of perfection. For a Christian, that perfection is Jesus Christ because He is truly, in the eyes of a Christian, the example of what a man and woman should strive to be. I have found that in studying the life of Jesus Christ, that so many of us who claim to be Christians could not even express in a cognitive way what the role of Jesus Christ would look like in today's society. How can you mirror the very perfection you are supposed to be if you do not understand how perfection actually existed? Then how could you show that perfection in your own way of living if you don't understand it?

It's very important that that image in yourself be portrayed the correct way. I'm not asking anyone to become Jesus. I'm not asking anyone to attempt to become Jesus. What I'm asking everyone to take a look at the example that Jesus set then look at yourself and see where you can tighten up the areas in your life that you know need repair. If that leads you to a path where you start to emulate and become like Jesus, that's a good thing in my eyes.

I am nowhere near where I would like to be. I believe that there is still so much more growth that I have to achieve and my studying is going to continue so I can get there. I settled on the title, "From Gigolo to Jesus," because I want people to understand the extreme transition my life has taken. I would be a fool to believe I can become Jesus Christ, but I'm not crazy to think that I can become the best K. L. that I can be. I think if anyone of us set out each day to try to be as perfect as we could for ourselves, the world would be so much better. If we all stepped out with the mindset of just trying to be as good as we can within everything that we do, there is no way this world stays the same.

Paying For Your Sins

When you grow in your faith there has to be accountability for your behavior. That lesson transcends across all of the different faiths. You can't live your life negatively and not expect that there be some type of penalties. As a Christian, you learn that the wages of sin is death, but I think people take it too general. We all know that once we are born we are destined to die, but have you ever thought of death as being more than the end of our physical being?

Death doesn't have to be instantaneous. There are personal concessions many do not realize are going to be made. Subconsciously, you're in turmoil and have not recognized that there is even a problem. For example, because I didn't have a father I grew distrust for people. I was afraid that eventually a woman would treat me like I treated others. I lost the comfort of knowing that when I'm with someone who has my best interest, I didn't have to fear anything. Essentially, I had a fear of being in a loving relationship. So I did everything to try to avoid it in order to not be hurt.

Also, there's financial death. After creating multiple children with multiple women I have a moral and legal obligation to take care of them. This means that I work hard, but often struggle to make ends meet because more than seventy-five percent of my income goes toward child support. I don't have expendable income for luxuries. I'm happy just barely being able to put food on the table and keep a roof over my head. Are you getting the picture? Death doesn't mean you just fall over and that's it.

The beauty of transitioning is to know there is light at the end of the tunnel. I have allowed myself to fall in love and be faithful to my wife, Tiffany. We have a supportive and nurturing relationship. My child support requirements will begin to decrease starting in seven years. Three years after will completely end my financial obligations. This will allow me to set goals for our future. Before learning my role as a Christian I used to be angry at the amount of money that never reached my hands. I used to be like some men who ask: "Is it really necessary to have that much for child support?"

There's also the death of privacy. Choosing to be with so many women meant choosing to share information that should have been shared with just my wife. There are women who have an intimate knowledge of me that they don't deserve. That means they share something with my wife that they should never have had, and I have to live with that. I try to make up for that by loving my wife dearly, and with everything I have inside of me. She knows what she has is greater than anything other women can hold. Yes, they may know about me sexually, but they will never have felt what it is to have unadulterated love with me.

We push to make sure that love between us is unwavering. My wife means that much to me and so I make a habit that wherever I go, I talk about the role she plays in my life. I try to be transparent so folks can understand I regret the life that I lived before her, but I cannot change the past. Instead I live to enjoy what my wife brings to our marriage.

There's also the death of being comfortable in a public setting. I have put myself in a position where my past constantly interrupts my life. Several times my wife and I encountered women I have been with. I have no choice, but to acknowledge them, although some don't want to acknowledge me. Some just look and my wife will ask, "Why is she looking at you/me that way?"

I'm very honest with her when it comes to my previous affairs. There have been so many women that have asked, "Did you tell your wife about us?" The answer is yes. There has been no exemption. I feared if I didn't arm Tiffany with the information then someone would make a feeble attempt to use it as a weapon against us. For the most part, we have talked about how we may bump into my past many times along the road. We've even discussed the possibility of someone knocking on the door saying that I am their father. In fact our family has grown by two since we began dating ten years ago—both children were conceived prior to our relationship, of course.

When people live a sinful life they do not consider the death of their soul. There have been many discussions on life after death. If you're a Christian, like me, you are taught that how you live your life will determine the destiny of your soul. The fear of any devout Christian is that they leave this eternal plane before having an opportunity to make amends for the life they chose to live. Life is considered a gift and how you use that gift will make a statement on how you view the faith. I'm not going to get into that any further. However, we are so similar in how we have chosen to live our lives that if we would discuss just the mistakes we would have a better understanding of how to make better choices in our lives.

As we get older and think back on things we could have changed because we didn't like their outcomes we would possibly rewrite our whole story. We can attribute most of it to our naiveté. I chalk most of it up to youth which many of us have to. The few of us who are lucky enough to have reached an age where we can acknowledge the results of those choices utter the well famous statement "If I could go back." Well there is no going back. However, in going forward, the hope is that you learned a tremendous amount from the person that you were and then draw a line in the sand with a vow that you're not going to go back to being that person.

The only way to get to that point is to be transparent in admitting who you were. Many do not want to do that, but I do it on a regular basis with my students, friends, colleagues, and even with strangers on the street. Anywhere I believe my testimony is going to help I'm going to offer the truth about what I was and discuss who I am now because there are people out here who need someone they can turn to for answers. Especially when they believe you may share something in common. They need to be able to sit down and look me in the face and say, let me ask you a question: When you were cheating on your wife, did you worry about her feelings? I have to look them right in their eyes and honestly respond, "At the time, no." The truth is I worried about her feelings when I came in the home. I wasn't worried about her feelings when fulfilling the acts. I understand I open myself up to ridicule, but I think it's important to have that dialogue and to be able to explain to people where my mind frame was. I am direct with people when I tell them I didn't love myself and part of me wanted to die. People need to be able to sit down and look at you because they're looking for empathy in order to be able to offer their own wisdom.

As an educator, I notice that kids want to know that it's okay before they put their problems on the table. They want to share without being persecuted. Their behaviors dictate to me when something is wrong. I don't react to the behavior because the behavior is just a means to get my attention. Once they have my attention it's time to dig for what is causing the problem. I look at it as the headache syndrome. When you have a headache, the headache is not the problem. The headache is the result of a problem. You can treat the headache but if you don't treat the cause, the headache will come back. I have to deal with the same thing in school and hence I had to deal with the same thing in my life as well as in others' lives when they come to confide in me. If I only deal with the behaviors then we're not dealing with what's actually behind the scenes.

In discussions I tell people that I hated myself because I was unhappy with my weight gain, my failures, the demise of my first marriage, having so many children, and not having any money. I was unhappy with so many different things that it didn't change until I took ownership of my unhappiness. Many folks do not want to do that. They don't want to admit they are the cause of what is going wrong with them. It's easier to blame others because then there is no reason for them to change who they are.

At a very young age men are taught not to express their feelings. An emotional man is considered "soft" so most of us will allow ourselves to die on the inside because we don't know how to ask for help. Some men define themselves by their pain. Some feel that without pain, they can't be a man. Young men are taught don't ever admit weakness because then the world will take advantage of you. If these are the messages our young men are receiving, then we are not teaching them the right ways of how to be men.

I press upon the young men I teach on a daily basis to be mindful of the decisions they make. Now I use a lot of clichés, I hate to say it, but I do because they fit. I say to them all the time, the bed that you make right now, you'll have to lay in and if you fill that bed with nails or fill that bed with glass, that's the pain you're going to endure until you make a new bed. Then I ask do they want to do that? I tell them to use my knowledge at forty-three-years-old to give themselves twenty-plus years of a head start on their own future. I tell them to make their future so much better than it could be simply by saying, 'I am going to get to a point where Mr. B could never have gotten simply because I'm starting now.' That's how I offset some of the problems that these young men may have to go through.

I try to give so much of myself that they don't have to face any of the negativity to the degree that I have. Now, they're going to make their mistakes, but if more of us step up and offer our truth, the deaths that have come from the choices we've made well then we have now allowed others to benefit and grow. It's so important. So, my goal has been to offer a lifeline. Just like on "Who Wants to Be a Millionaire" when you're sitting there, you have a question to answer, and you really don't have the answer.

Another aspect of why I'm transparent and why I try to help is our older male generation appears to be in a state of ultra denial. They take their pain and act as if it's not even real. They just get up and go through the daily routine in whatever form or fashion that it's going to be and they simply discount what the past was. Some don't even consider it as a tool to learn from. It's done, it's over and I'm focusing on what I'm doing today. There is no learning so there is no change. A lot of older brothers would love to turn around and get it right. Some don't believe they can. If you have a man in his forties or fifties who believes he cannot change, imagine how much damage he can do to himself and to anyone connected to him? It's sad to say a lot of men have never been taught how to be humble.

Being a man is held like a badge of honor and in this society, we tend to connect being humble with something degrading. The minute that you talk about humility; the minute that you talk about conceding to someone else, you're considered soft. So I'm not shocked that young men don't understand this because older men are not teaching it and they don't even want to recognize it.

The first time many young men learn humility is through sports. They learn that things are just not going to happen the way you want all of the time. You have to give in to the team. You have to give in to the coach. In some cases you have to give in to the opponent. The great coaches seem to understand that there's a time to be humble and there's a time when not to be, but how many great coaches do our children really get to directly observe?

Overall, in the grand scheme of things, we have generations of young men being taught from older men nothing that's even remotely connected to humility. I am offering with my writing and with everything else that I have in my life a way to accept that being humble is not a negative quality. I am six feet and four hundred plus pounds. I ask my students, "Does anything about me look soft?" If I then point out to them, if there's nothing about me that seems out of the ordinary in your eyes and I tell you that it's ok to practice humility, then how could it be a bad thing? It at least starts the conversation towards change.

Something else I've noticed with older men which flows down to our younger men is the lack of empathy. Identifying with and understanding someone else's feeling, especially those of another man, is often characterized as homosexual. I don't see empathy being practiced regularly. On occasion you will find it during sports or during some type of conflict when a mediator has to get involved. The mediator becomes the impartial witness being able to listen to all sides and then relay messages that may fall short. I encounter parents who come to the school and have no empathy for children other than their own. Then I have parents who have no empathy for their own children. Often, I hear "I don't care. He/she has to learn." Parents don't even want to hear what the circumstances are. You start to think to yourself, my God if they go home to this every day, now I understand why the child acts they way they do.

As you're reading, if you're thinking what can I do to be a better role model for my children or who can I look for in my neighborhood or in my community? First and foremost, look for men in the church, men in school, men in your local community organizations who are working on developing the community. Learn about events in your area so that you can take time to meet them in a relaxed setting where you can explain what your goals and the goals of your son are. This way you can see if there is compatibility. You will start to come in contact with men of valor, men of honor, men who have the intestinal fortitude that you want your young men to be like. I would also say to look for older men who still hold the traditional values of what men are supposed to be.

Having open dialogues with people who share your interests is a great way to build your support system. As often as possible I would suggest talking with as many folks in the same circumstances as you. Seek out message boards, social networks on the internet, and even look for other parents in your child's school that will be mutually beneficial. Discuss what has and hasn't worked. That way you don't have to waste your time going in a direction that won't give you results. This way you also now have an opportunity to really sit down and build the foundation for possible alternatives to what you might be dealing with.

When I travel, I come across so many parents who say, "I wish you could come and teach at my school." I appreciate it. Don't get me wrong. I am grateful every time I hear a parent say that they would love to have me become their child's educator, but I know that there are other good men out here. There are great people who are a living example of what you want for your son.

You have to find a way to meet them, talk with them and build a foundation with them where there is communication.

When I stand in front of an audience and discuss the things I've talked about in this book many of them are shocked. Once they get past the shock, now we can get down to the actual help. Now we can get to what can be done to change the situation that they're in. You can see the approval from the conversation because they can't wait until the speaking engagement is over so they can ask questions and exchange contact information. They share with me what their sons and daughters are going through. I try to offer options they may not have considered. It's not just about selling books. It's about using these books to create opportunities to talk to folks and actually help people. I know that's a rare thing. I know that a lot of people say it, but I really do live it. I love when people come to me and they want to converse about making changes. I look forward to it.

I am delighted that you picked up this book. I am even more moved if you have read this far. I thank you for giving me the opportunity to share my testimony, but I really want to stress something to you before you move on. There are answers to every question. There is help for every situation. I don't care how old a person is; how negative they may seem, there is a way to reach them. You may have to search out a few different ways until you come up with the right answers, but it's out there.

Also, don't be scared to pray. Never be scared just to sit back close your eyes and ask the Lord to assist you and how to go about reaching that person in your life who can't seem to change. My grandmother, God bless her, I still have her in my life and she has never stopped praying for me. She has never stopped offering me advice on the best way to go about things. I have a Master's Degree yet I still reach out to my grandmother to ask her for her advice because her life experiences have matched up with my degree. The life experiences of my mother and grandmother allow me to digest more. Listening to them helps me.

Our families need for young and older men to come back to the table and take their places inside their families. Some would say back at the head of the table and I would agree. We need our males to come back into the picture, come back and look to repair their families like I did my own and then those wages against their sins would decrease. There's still going to be some payment to be made and time lost, but the minute that they decide to turn and do better there's going to be some repair. There's going to be some love and there's going to be some happiness that can come back even if it's for a short amount of time. I believe that it's worth it even if it's only for a day. People need to know that type of feeling and I hope that now as you have gotten to the end of this chapter, you are motivated to go out and begin to create the foundation; motivated to go out and assist someone in that change.

It may not happen overnight but it can happen rather quickly if you put the time in. It has to start somewhere. You took the time out to read this book, why not let it start with you?

My Growing Family

Until we can see tangible evidence it is often difficult to recognize the ultimate blessing from making necessary changes in our lives. One of the blessings is connecting or reconnecting with family. For me it's both. One of the beauties of finding myself was that it caused me to come home and take a deeper look at the woman that was in my life. The woman that had put up with my foolishness and who had been in my corner from the moment I met her and that's my wife, Tiffany.

I caught heat from one of the mother's of my children when I wrote in my first book, "A Man In Transition", that Tiffany is the most important person in my life. According to the mother my children should have come first. Some of you may agree with her, but I stand by what I wrote. This is the reason why I recognize her first in this chapter. I have already explained Tiffany was the guiding force and support system that helped me realize I needed to be a better man and a better father. I had to get myself together and learn to love myself, first, before I could be any good to anyone, including my children.

Think about how many women sit by condoning their partner's foolish behavior. Girlfriends and wives accepting that their partner has children they don't have a relationship with nor pay child support for. Tiffany wasn't having it. Don't think I didn't try to pull the wool over her eyes on occasion. When dealing with my children's mothers if I was wrong she would let me know, and would even have the nerve to tell me that she thought I should apologize in some instances. That showed me she wasn't going to follow whatever I said blindly. It also let me know that she was more concerned about right and wrong than taking up for me just because I was her man. On the other hand when I was right she backed me all the way, but would still give me advice on how to handle situations in the most diplomatic way. Her concerns above all were always how my children were going to be affected. She says, often, "I don't care about the feelings of the adults. It's time for all of you to grow up because there are children involved; it's no longer about you."

She hung in there as I transitioned. She saw enough in me to want me to be her husband. We tend to forget that when we take a spouse, the way marriage was designed, the two of you are now a new and combined entity. Your extended families are now connected because of the marriage, but the bond you two share is something that is totally separate from both sides of the family.

I have found our abilities as one solid unit are much greater than what either one of us could do alone. Who I was before I reconnected with my wife is nothing compared to the blessings that came after I reconnected with her. I believe Tiffany assisted in saving my life. Learning to humble myself; learning to give in to the softer side of the male persona; trusting a woman that was in my life at that moment; trusting that she had a better understanding of things she saw than I had given her credit for and then allowing our faith to be a guide became the sealing bond that, to this day, allows us to go out and be among people and talk about the things that went on in the past. It is almost magical to watch the eyes of women when I tell them how much I love my wife. It is incredible to watch the way people react when they see us together and they tell us we look so much in love. Well, we are. There is no reason to sugar coat it or hide it.

In my years of studying the Bible, I have learned that Jesus is an example of what we can strive to be. We can't be perfect and everyone understands that. However, once you have a blueprint of what you can become and then you have a woman in your life that's willing to take those same steps with you, your faith grows; your mutual respect for each other strengthens. Your relationship becomes secure. In fact, I don't worry about the next man moving in and getting past our defenses.

Tiffany and I seem to balance each other out. Her strengths are my weaknesses and her weaknesses are my strengths. Even with the company we have created together we have taken responsibilities that help to maximize our abilities to grow it. She handles some of the editing and creative development as well as offers ideas on where she sees the company going. I handle the technological, financial, and contractual aspects. When we come together, we develop a quality product; better than either one of us could put together alone and that is what the essence of an incredibly positive marriage is about. Being something better together than you could ever be by yourself.

So as you're reading this, understand that part of the blessing that goes back to finding God and repairing things with Tiff, now leads me to circumstances that I don't know how I would have been able to deal with on my own. My life was taking on a whole new direction. Something I had never seen before and as I stated earlier, as doors closed, new doors began to open. People say that often, but they don't take the time to pay attention to that very fact going on in their life. As you carve away the negative entities that are zapping your life of its energy, God will send you to people that you need that will not only restore your energy but will take you by the hand and take you places that you didn't consider and when you get there, you'll reap the benefits of what you've gained by getting to the new plateau.

Throughout this book I have discussed the affects of not having my father or a positive male fixture in my life. Even after accomplishing so much without my father it never stopped my longing to meet the man that I heard so much about. Every time I visit Penns Grove, New Jersey people would say, 'I just saw your father' or 'You look so much like your father.' I don't think I can begin to explain what it feels like for everyone around you to know and have seen your father, but you have never laid eyes on him.

I remember receiving an email from my aunt Noonie—my father's sister. She got my email address from my half brother, Derwin. She wrote that I should reach out to my father because both of us seemed to be stubborn and we needed to find each other and talk. I wrote back I can't be stubborn with someone I've never met. I told her I would love to reach out and know who he is, but I've never had the opportunity. My aunt forwarded me all his information and wrote, "You two need to get this done."

So, I sat and thought about it. I talked to my wife and I asked her, "What should I do?" My wife said, "The Lord has presented you with an opportunity to reconnect with your father. You should take it." That's something else that my wife and I share. We both come from homes where the men who called themselves our fathers—our biological fathers—were men who just made multiple children with different women and were not a part of our lives. I knew Tiff would understand what I was feeling.

I sat and stared at the email for a while and then decided it can't hurt. I prayed about it. I typed up a nice email explaining who I was. I shared with him that I was an educator, I told him about my children, and my wife. I attached pictures of his grandchildren and his daughter-in-law and me. One of the things that I made sure I put in the email was that I apologized to him for any negative feelings that I had towards him and also stated that I understood if allowing me to walk into his life now would cause difficulty. I told him he did not have to respond because I no longer hold a grudge against him. My father read the email and he was so blown away by it he felt it his duty to respond to me.

My father had had his own epiphany with the Lord many years earlier, had changed his life and was living much better than he was in the past. In his email he told me how touched he was that I had reached out to him. He respected the fact that I said if this was going to be a problem in his life, that it was ok if he didn't respond.

We talked for a while, but it didn't seem long enough. He then told me he wanted me to do a DNA test before we went further. He had seen circumstances where people showed up and claimed to be someone's child and it turn out not to be the case. Some people would have been offended because he had been with my mom and everyone said we looked alike. However, it makes sense to be certain before he disrupted his and his family's life with something that may not be true. I didn't have a problem with it because I had gone through it with one of my own children. There are circumstances that arise which you know although there is a possibility that you fathered a child you weren't in the most trustworthy circumstances. So he sent the exam in the mail. I did a swab and got the results back a few weeks later that it was 99% positive I was his son.

I love my father because the minute he found out and got the confirmation, he instantly turned the love on. I think he already felt in his heart that I was his son, but he needed that reassurance.

At forty-years-old, exactly three weeks before my marriage to Tiffany, I met my father for the first time. I remember Tiffany helping me pack and saying, "See if you can convince him to come to the wedding." I still wasn't sure how I was going to feel about meeting him or how he would feel about meeting me. The last thing on my mind was inviting him to the wedding. In my mind I was thinking what if he really didn't want to have anything to do with me after all this time? What if our meeting rehashed some hard feeling that couldn't get resolved?

My brother, Derwin and I, both, were concerned about meeting our father. Derwin is older than me by a couple of months. Yes, that means my father had two young ladies pregnant at the same time. We learned we were brothers in high school when our opposing teams competed against each other. Someone who knew both of our parents said, "Hey do you know you guys are brothers?" We kept in contact ever since.

Now my brother's anger was a little different from mine. He wasn't too keen on the idea of meeting our father for the first time in almost 40 years. He felt that no excuse could be made for abandoning your children.

The night before we met our father we were in the bar and I remember telling Derwin, "Listen, we don't say anything. Let him say what he has to say. We'll listen and we'll take it from there." I could see his dismay. We decided to call it an early night. I went back to the hotel. He went home.

The next day, my father called and wanted to know what hotel I was staying in. I was staying at the Comfort Inn. He said, "We should be there in a few minutes." He told me he was staying in Delaware which is maybe fifteen to twenty minutes from where I was in South Jersey. I thought we were going to meet somewhere neutral in public for our first meeting. About fifteen minutes later there was a knock at the door I walked to the door and asked, "Who?" He replied, "It's Elijah Causey, your father." I've since learned that my father is a straight up guy as I said before so it wasn't just Elijah. He said his whole name and stated his role. Not a problem. I opened the door, there's this man standing about six foot three, slightly older looking, a little gray, medium build. We locked eyes, he stepped into the room, he shook my hand and said, "How you doing, son?" I've never said this to anyone. I was as excited as a grown man could be, however, I knew I had to keep my composure because there were still some emotional issues I was dealing with, but I was happy. My whole life I lived without a father now I was standing in front of him.

We hugged. Then he came into the room and sat on the couch. I sat in a chair across from him and we got to talking. We must have talked for a good hour and then I realized I can't do this alone. There was somebody else that was supposed to be enjoying this with me so I called my brother to come down to the hotel. He whispered in the phone, "Is he there?" I said, "Yes sir. Come on."

When Derwin arrived all of us talked for about three hours. We sat and listened as our father explained why he had not been there for us. He said it was my email that moved him to want to walk through that door. He told us that he thought our respective mothers had placed poison in the water, and I'm not saying that literally I mean mental poison, against him or about whom he was so he had figured going on with his life was the best thing for everyone.

I can't speak for my brother, but I could see the look on his face and see that he was as giddy as I was to have our father there. When I listened to his story about the choices he made when he was younger shaping what he was now at sixty-years-old I was hearing my own story. He was telling *my* story in *his* life. I was overwhelmed, but I held it together.

At that moment, I let go of any negative feelings I had towards my father. How could I hate him when he had lived the life I was currently living? How can I dislike someone who made some of the similar choices that I made? Though there were some choices that he made that I would have done differently. I wouldn't have left completely and not contacted my children, but I understood why he made the choice. There was no way I could dislike him.

To hear my father say he went to church and he prayed that we were doing well and to hear him say he was happy and sad at the same time was heartwarming. I asked him why and he said, "I'm happy to see that you two have grown to be two fine young men but I'm sad that I wasn't there to be a part of it." Then he asked, "Do you want to go meet your brother and your stepmother? They're here in the hotel."

My father wasn't staying in Delaware. We were staying in the same hotel. I understood he had to be careful, but I had to laugh. So we all took a walk, actually, up one flight and down the hallway. We went in and I met my stepmother, Marie. Marie is a full-figured, light skinned woman and I found it funny that all three of us have affection for full-figured women. I met my youngest brother who also looks like my father with a lighter complexion. We all seemed to have my father's large head.

I realized my father and I had a lot more in common. We both have the same number of children. One of my sons and my father share the same name. It wasn't intentional. Not knowing my father, I actually named my son after Malcolm X. My father and I have sons the same age. Yes, my dad was still getting it on. His wife is nine years younger than him. My wife is nine years younger than me. Both of our wives keep blankets in the car during the summer because they don't like air conditioning. We both were married in the month of August and honeymooned in Jamaica, West Indies. My father and I are both night owls.

When I invited my father to my wedding he wasn't sure if he could make it. He had planned a vacation to begin that same weekend and the truth was he was still apprehensive because he hadn't seen my mom and grandmother since before I was born. He wasn't sure what type of atmosphere he would be walking into.

I'm thankful to say my father rearranged his schedule and he, my stepmother, and brother joined us on that day. When I look at my wedding video and see my father dancing with my mother it still makes me smile. For the first time since I was born my father was sharing an important moment in my life. He had not been there for graduations, sports events, birthdays, and the birth of his grandchildren, but he made sure he was there for my wedding.

It's been over three years and my father and I have talked regularly, and I have visited him at his home multiple times. He has met his grandchildren. We've celebrated birthdays, anniversaries, and holidays. I honestly believe that the Lord knew that I was going to need him in my forties more than I did when I was younger because the advice that he is giving me in my life since we've met has been invaluable. Because my father has similar experiences I can go to him as my sounding board and an anchor to decisions that I make with my children and wife. I can only thank God for knowing that I was going to need him now.

My children are the results of decisions that I've made but I don't begrudge any of them. When I look back on my past, would I change how I lived my life? Of course, this book would not be written if I didn't want to change some of the things I've done. However, my children being here, I love them and I deal with my responsibilities the best I can. Meeting my father prepared me to meet my twenty-five year old son, Jonathan, for the first time in 2009. Jonathan's mother told me more than once that I was not his father. I later found out that her fear of me kept her from telling me the truth.

I'm proud to say that he is a member in the armed services and is a 9/11 hero, who was recognized by the Mayor of New York City for saving the life of a police officer during the terrorist attacks. He was studying to be an EMT at the time and when his classmates were running away from the devastation he was running toward it to offer his assistance. When all of the EMTs, police, and other civilians sought shelter in a nearby church there was an officer lying outside in the street as debris was falling around him.

Jonathan made the decision to leave the safety of the church to save the officer's life. Understand there's no way for Jonathan to know what was going on around him at the time because no one knew but he just knew the police officer needed help. Jonathan carried the officer into the church. That particular officer worked in the Mayors' office. For his gratitude the officer helped Jonathan go to college.

Although Jonathan did not know me when he lived in the complex I grew up in people would always tell him that he looked like someone named Keith. He kept wondering who I was and asked his mom and aunts about me. They admitted to him that there might be a chance that I was his father.

I'm going to show you how the Lord works and how some things are just not coincidence. There was a time when Jonathan only lived a block away from where I lived with my first wife. He also graduated, in the summer, from the Junior High School I began teaching in the fall of that same year. My friends and colleagues were his teachers. Our paths were crossing all of the time. I could have looked right at him when he was a little boy not realizing he was my son.

Jonathan's aunt reached out to me in the summer of 2009 and revealed to me that I was Jonathan's father. He wanted to meet me, but was a little nervous because he wasn't sure how I was going to take finding out after all that time. I said, "Man listen. Tell him to call me", and I gave her my number. When he called I told him the same thing that my father said to me. "All I can offer you is love and answers." To hear his excitement; to feel his positive energy; to hear his story, shook my soul.

When I finally got a chance to meet him, all I could do was just look at him because he looked just like me. He looked just like my other children. My family welcomed him right away as if he has always been with us. Since meeting we have only seen each other a few times, but we speak on the phone and through Facebook. He is a very active young man and as I said he's enlisted in the service. He's now serving on a submarine.

This past school year, he actually came to my job to visit me. It was great that my students had a chance to meet him because I talk about him often. It also helped tremendously with my young men's group at the school when they got to listen to my son tell his 9/11 story. We are growing and we're going to continue to grow. As time progresses, we're going to get to know each other even more. It's just a blessing to have him in my life as my son and I don't care about the circumstances surrounding how we connected. I'm just glad that we have each other. I know he appreciates it as much as I do.

My second oldest child, Kierra is twenty-one-years old. I spoke about her in a previous chapter. She was also a child that I did not find out about until after she was born. I think of all my children my relationship with Kierra is the most volatile. It wasn't her fault that she came during a time when I wasn't prepared to be a father. Are there things I would have done differently in order for us to have a better relationship? Of course.

In hindsight, the first mistake I made was to let another man attempt to raise my daughter. It was one of the biggest mistakes I have made in my life. The second mistake is when Kierra moved back to New York, after her grandfather passed away, when she was almost eleven years old. A decision was made to have Kierra live with an aunt and uncle on her mother's side of the family instead of living with her mother. At that point I should have realized there was no reason I should continue to allow someone else to raise my daughter. I often think how different things would be if I would have stepped up, and told her mother that if Kierra wasn't going to live with her then she would live with me, but I didn't. What child wouldn't be hurt when he or she has two capable parents who should be caring for them, but instead is living with other family members. Kierra lived like an orphan, but wasn't one.

One of the things my relationship with Kierra has also taught me is that when a man creates children with multiple women, he may want to love all of his children and he will do that, but he will not be able to love all of them the same way. He can try. There are so many factors that influence the relationship. I made that mistake with Kierra because she was here in New York; she was close and I didn't put the effort in because I was married and trying to take care of what was my next family. I can understand how she felt because I was in her shoes once, when I was younger when I felt that family didn't want me. I don't have to imagine what it felt like to her to think I didn't want her. After all I didn't think my father wanted me. It created a great chasm between my daughter and me and it only grew worse as the years passed.

As Kierra got older she began to rebel. It was as if I was looking at myself growing up. She was angry at how her stepfather treated her mother and shared that with me. She felt helpless and as her father I didn't do much to remove her pain. I would just send her back into the lion's den. I'm now paying for that mistake. I wrote a poem in my first book titled, "I'm Not Superman, I'm Dad." When I look back I realize there are many occasions that Kierra needed me to be Dad and I ignored them. I wanted her to be someone else's problem. It eventually became my problem when Kierra's mother decided she had enough. Kierra had run away from home multiple times, she had skipped school so many days, and I didn't find out until later that she had even been in some legal trouble. So the decision was made that she would live at my parent's house when she was sixteen.

At the time, Tiff and I lived in Brooklyn and when I think about it we had enough space for her to come live with us, but once again I was allowing someone else to be a parent to my daughter. Tiff even said on more than one occasion that she should live with us. I have to give Tiffany credit for being wise beyond her years. She told me she understood how Kierra felt. Although Tiffany had her stepfather, who she praises often for the way he raised her, she still had animosity toward her biological father that abandoned her and her brother when they were very young. Tiffany told me in Kierra's sixteen years she didn't have stability which is something she needed. She needed to have family structure, but most of all she needed to feel loved and wanted by her father. I should have listened to Tiffany.

While my daughter lived with my parents I still didn't make the time to connect which only caused things to get worse. She started practicing an alternative lifestyle and she began dating girls. I believe this, too, was her way of rebelling. This was her way of getting some type of attention even if it was negative. One decision I did make was to change her school to one within walking distance from my parent's house. It would have also removed her from the negative influences she had encountered. However, instead of taking my place as her father to make sure she was registered in the new school I left it to my grandmother.

My daughter begged and convinced my grandmother to let her stay in her old school. Once again, I was allowing someone else to remove my authority as her father. I wasn't being respected, as her father, by her nor my own parents. So the reality is I was only a father in theory.

In November 2007, Kierra was eighteen-years-old. Unknown to us she and a group of her friends assaulted a man on the train. Another young lady who filmed the attack from her cell phone put the video on Youtube. The "A Train Beat Down" video quickly swept around the country and made its way to the news. Her mother called me and asked "Have you watched the news?" I said, "No." When I did get a chance to watch there was my daughter verbally assaulting a man and being very disrespectful. At the end of the tirade that group of young women swarmed around the young man and physically assaulted him.

When I asked my daughter why, she said, "Dad you don't understand. The man threatened us. The man was trying to harm us." I said, "Well let me go back and watch the video because maybe I'm missing something." I watched the video a second time and I did not see any of what she was saying. I saw a man making an attempt to leave before the altercation and then being pushed by one of the assailants and told, "You're not going anywhere."

The next day while I was at work I had a conversation with a young lady who had gotten into some trouble. I said to her, "You really need to tell your parents what you did." She said, "But Mr. B, if I go home and tell my mother what I did, I'm going to get into so much trouble. I'm going to get a beating." I said, "Sweetheart you can never be nervous about telling the truth because the truth has to be told regardless of the outcome. Your parents don't want to find out that you did something wrong from some other way when you could tell them yourself."

As I was going home that day I thought about what I told that student. I thought to myself, 'How can I tell my students to do the right thing and then turn a blind eye to this horrific act that my daughter committed? The first thing I did was call the New York City Police Department. I explained to them who I was and the detective in charge of the case told me until the crime was actually reported there was nothing they could do. He said with the information he had they could begin to investigate and take it a step further.

I then called the New York Daily News which had already written an article about the incident. When I called them, the phone rang, someone picked up on the other end, and I hung up the phone. I guess they have Caller ID because they called me right back. They asked me if I called and I asked, "Who's handling the report with the assault on the A Train?" The woman I was speaking with told me she was.

"Does anyone know any information about the young ladies on the video?" I asked her.

"Yes, we're gaining information now because we want to bring this crime to justice."

"Well, I can tell you about one of the young ladies. I'm her father."

The reporter was blown away. "You're the father?"

"Yes. I'm going to give you all of my daughter's information. Whatever happens, happens because what I watched on television was wrong."

"Well, we're going to have someone call you back if you don't mind."

Sure enough, later on that night, the reporter called and we did an interview over the phone. It was printed in the New York Daily News the next day. When Kierra's mother called me the next day she was livid. There was no conversation just ranting and raving about how I could do this to her daughter. She wanted to know why we couldn't just handle this in the family between us. It was as if Kierra's behavior in the past years had not gotten progressively worse no matter what was tried. I asked her, "Has Kierra been arrested before?"

Kierra's mother had previously shared with Tiffany that Kierra had been detained by police for disorderly conduct. Tiff didn't share the information with me until the train incident. When I asked Tiffany why she didn't tell me she said, "When Kierra's mother told me I thought she would have told you shortly after. When she didn't I felt she was trying to use me to tell you instead of addressing it with you herself. As Kierra's mother, if she didn't feel it important enough to discuss with you then I wasn't going to play the fall guy." Tiffany realized she had developed a trusting bond with Kierra. If it was thought that Tiffany had betrayed that trust by revealing that information to me, then her mother would appear like the "good guy" and Tiffany would be the evil stepmother that wanted to see Kierra in trouble.

The question obviously caught Kierra's mother off guard. She hesitated and then responded, "What, what does that have to do with anything?" I thought I heard it all until she asked, "Is that man on the train more important than your daughter?"

When I spoke to my daughter, again, I asked her, "What are we going to do to make this right?" She said, "I will do whatever I need to do to make this right." I said, "Okay, when the detectives come to contact you, I want that to be the case because I gave them the information." She gasped, "What?" She became upset and hung up the phone. It was more proof to me that she was not ready to be held accountable for her actions. This was something else she thought would be eventually swept under the rug like so many other offenses.

The following day the NY Daily News produced an interview with the gentleman from the train who was now going to press charges. This meant there was a possibility my daughter was going to go to jail. Did I want to see my daughter in jail? Not at all, but I was afraid that if some tough love wasn't imparted she would become out of control. I got a call from CNN to come and do the Rick Sanchez show. I had just done an interview with Channel 12, which is Brooklyn News, from my house so I decided to do the CNN interview also.

I only had one agenda. We often hear people ask, "What type of parents are raising their children to be out on the train beating someone up?" or "Where were the parents?" I wanted to let the world know her mother and I weren't the best parents, but we also were not what everybody was thinking—the worst.

When I was on the Rick Sanchez show, we had a great conversation about my daughter, but the one question he asked that stood out was, "Are you mad at her?" I guess he was expecting me to say, hell yeah I'm mad at her, but I said, "No, I'm sad *for* her because I know she knows better." When I saw the reaction in his face, he was literally blown away because he was expecting so much negativity to come from me.

This happened after I found the Lord and was I calm. The situation was actually a blessing. I hoped someone would see the interview and offer some type of help and I did get that offer. A female officer from the Brooklyn Borough President's Office called and said, "Once all this is situated, if you'd like somebody to come and maybe sit down with your daughter, I would love to because I just think it's a beautiful thing what you did in trying to get her some help."

Afterwards all the local news started to rebroadcast my interview on CNN. My daughter was kicked out of my parent's home and for over a year, we didn't talk. I would see her status messages on the internet and they were so very negative. There was no remorse. There was no personal accountability. In her eyes she didn't do anything all that bad and according to her attitude she was wronged. Thankfully, after a few court appearances she only received probation—no jail time.

I knew our relationship was going to be very difficult to repair and now three years later; it's still not where it should be. How will it be repaired? I don't know. My daughter has since moved back into my house and we both live under the same roof, but we rarely ever say anything other than "Hello" and "Goodbye" to each other.

I'm proud that she has made changes in her life. Since the incident she received her GED, she is working, and plans to start college soon. She aspires to be a singer or do something in the entertainment industry. In time, I believe like anything else, wounds will heal. I hope they will.

One day, when she's older or has children of her own she will realize that for the first time in her life, I was a responsible father. It wasn't the ideal circumstance, but I believe if I had continued to hope for things to fix themselves my daughter would be in a worse state. People may not agree with the choice I made, but I did what I thought was best for my daughter and I will accept the sacrifice of not having that father-daughter relationship if that means saving her life.

My son, Anthony, born on Super Bowl Sunday 1992, was a product of my first marriage. What I find interesting is he seems to be torn between his mother and me. Anthony shares both of our characteristics—some more than others. At times, it has caused the rift between his mother and me to grow. When his mother and I separated he was eight years old. It took him about eight years to become comfortable with the idea that I wasn't coming back home. He was 16 years old when I asked him, "Did you think I was coming back home?" He said, "I thought you and mom would get back together." I knew it would be more difficult for him to adjust, compared to his younger brother Elijah, because he had been used to having a two-parent household.

Elijah was only four years old when I left. When I sat him and his brother down to explain that I was moving out of the house his biggest concern was whether they were going to see me anymore. Once I assured him that he would see me regularly he started to put together how he would benefit from me leaving.

"So, I'll have Christmas with you and I'll have Christmas with Mommy?"

"Yes."

"I'll have two Christmases?"

"Yes."

"Two birthdays?"

"Yes."

"Two homes?"

"Yes."

Elijah had already figured out that this didn't have to be a bad thing. He calculated he would receive twice as many gifts and twice as much love.

My second daughter is fourteen-years-old and the product of a relationship that should have never happened. I will refrain from using her name because the truth is she has no idea that I am her father. Her mother and I, both, were having an extramarital affair for a number of years. When she was born her mother would comment that she wasn't sure if her husband was the father and it was possible that I was. I never thought anything of it until the first time I saw a picture of her at about thirteen-years-old.

When I showed the picture to Tiffany she said, "Oh, my God that is definitely your daughter!" My daughter's mother has since separated from her husband and, unfortunately, that father-daughter relationship has also dissolved. My daughter's mother still does not want to tell her the truth about who I am. I have recently spoken to her and asked her does she have any idea when she is going to tell our daughter the truth. She said, "I will tell her when I think she's ready and I'm ready." I said to her, "I understand how you feel, but it really shouldn't have anything to do with you being ready because the longer you wait the harder it may be for her to deal with it and the more damage it can cause." She said, "I understand, but I'm going to wait until she's eighteen or older. So, unfortunately, I have to wait four or more years before Pandora's Box is opened, but there are so many things that concern me in this situation. For one, my daughter is being robbed of having a relationship with me and being welcomed into a loving family. Two, her mother is also taking a risk of destroying her own relationship with her daughter for keeping the truth from her. All I can do is pray that we will have a smooth outcome.

Last, but not least of my six children is Justin. He's ten years old. I met his mother when I was in college. Every man has met that one woman that if there was a sign on them that read: "AVOID THIS ONE!" you would keep walking right on by. I joke with Tiffany that she should have dated me in college then I wouldn't have gotten involved with Justin's mother. She said, "No, you would have just dated both of us."

In the beginning Justin's mother understood I was married with children. Like most affairs, I saw her whenever I could get time out of the house. I remember after a while things becoming really weird with her. She would get upset when I had to leave her house to go home. She started questioning my relationship with my wife, but that didn't stop me from making late night runs to her house.

In hindsight, if I would have known what I know now I would have seen the signs.

When Justin's mother told me she was pregnant with him I didn't think anything of telling her to go have an abortion. After all, this wasn't the first time that I got her pregnant—so I thought. I already knew having a baby while I was married was going to create a bigger problem than I was ready to handle. That's when Justin's mother revealed to me that she had lied about being pregnant by me before.

This is where Tiffany likes to remind me that men are so busy trying to get into the panties that they don't recognize "crazy". She didn't just lie about being pregnant. She actually created an entire lie including going to the clinic to have an abortion and even feigning being in pain from the procedure. She didn't want to have an abortion and insisted she was going to have the baby. There was nothing I could do. At that point I stopped seeing Justin's mother.

I remember receiving a couple of calls from her while she was pregnant. One was to invite me to the baby shower. I couldn't believe she was serious. What married man, in his right mind, would proudly attend the baby shower of his mistress? Even I wasn't that brazen. Then I remember getting a call from her to come to the hospital because she wanted me to sign the birth certificate. I told her no.

I didn't hear from her anymore for a few months until my mom, who shares the same first initial and last name as me, told me she received a call from family court. They were looking for me. When she presented me with the information, I said, "You know what? I'm going to take myself to court, turn myself in and put everything in place to pay child support." I realized if I didn't and I waited it could disrupt my future, his future and everybody involved.

It was at family court when I met Justin's grandmother for the first time. As my mistress there was no reason for us to meet each other's parents before that. I remember her mother sitting there with a very sad look on her face as I walked over to see my son for the first time. I apologized to her that we had to meet under those circumstances. Once we went into the court room, I asked for a paternity test because I remember Justin's mother telling me she had been dating other men at the time and with the fact that she admitted to lying about an abortion I wasn't sure what else she was capable of.

Asking for the paternity test caused ill feelings because Justin's mother thought I was being disrespectful, but I wasn't trying to be. I was being careful and invoking my right as a man which is what I was supposed to do. After the paternity test was finalized a child support order was put in place and it would be seven years before I saw my son again.

Justin's mother moved to Virginia and I was under the impression that she took my son with her. I didn't press the issue because I was dealing with my dissolving marriage. Justin and his mother being in Virginia became a solution to a problem.

After about a year, occasionally, I would receive calls from her telling me Justin was visiting his grandmother in New York and I should go pick him up. Just like that. Now most people would say well there was your opportunity to start a relationship with your son, but I honestly didn't trust Justin's mother. The truth is she didn't know anything about me other than I was some married guy she was sleeping with. I told her that if I was going to form a relationship with Justin then I thought she should be there for the first few times until he got comfortable with me. She insisted that she didn't want to be there when I came to get him. I don't know why any mother would want to send her child into a situation blindly and the last thing I wanted was to be accused of kidnapping or abuse so I just let it be.

Well, it wasn't until Justin was seven years old that I found out he was living in New York with his grandmother while his mother was living in Virginia. He was actually living only about fifteen minutes away from me. Believe it or not I wasn't mad at his mother. I was actually disappointed. By this time I had already started to get my life in order, Tiffany and I were engaged to be married, and I felt there was so much time wasted that I could have spent with him if his mother was honest with me. Only she knows why she chose to lie about where Justin was living, but it took another appearance in court and finally a mutual agreement in order to begin visits with my son. The past two and a half years have been great. Justin and I talk on the phone and he comes to visit. He is just one of the kids when he is with us.

So there you have my six children and their unique stories. I pray every day that I can be a better father to all of them. I owe them that much. It took me almost twenty years to realize and appreciate what being a father means. I haven't been perfect and haven't always made the best decisions, but I am willing to work to make things better.

Becoming a Writer

I never thought there was going to come a day when I would call myself a writer. Back in seventh grade I had an English teacher tell me, "I was the worst thing my mother ever had." I remember thinking to myself "I hate English and I hate Mr. _____.

The most difficult thing in the world is to become a writer when reading is not something you do for enjoyment. Now, don't get me wrong I do read, but curling up with a good book, for pleasure, is not my first choice. When I choose a book it's for knowledge and personal development.

Like many men, non-fiction, comics, and magazines will be at the top of list of my ready choices. However, what are you to do when the Lord places so much on your heart? When you're sitting around and so much is spilling out of your brain the only thing you can do is write. I am not a formally trained writer. In fact, if you asked my wife she would tell you that I leave a lot to be desired, but since I am an educator I do have a great understanding of how to get my point across. Then I hand it over to my wife for her to clean it up.

Reconnecting with my faith has taught me to listen to my inner voice and find avenues to get my thoughts out. Being expressive was never a problem for me. It's one of the first things you learn when you decide to become a lady's man. What woman wouldn't want a man who's able to reach inside her and pull forth the type of feelings that can drive her to sexual bliss? However, things are so different now. What I'm trying to do through my writing is drive home a message of comfort to my readers. I look at my writing as a vehicle to get through the emotions I deal with.

When I first began writing poetry I hid it from others because of the connection I had to my words. I would see things and scribble something down. When I was done, I would be scared to death to let anyone read it since it would give them unabated access to my soul.

Like all writers there is a personal connection to what's written. I simply hadn't learned to step back and allow someone else to enjoy my work. It was with my first book, a collection of poems, internet blogs and stories I wrote when I was in a totally different place mentally and spiritually. I took my wife's advice and allowed the world to see what I had inside my heart and the book was a success. It allowed me to walk through literary doors I wouldn't have thought were possible.

When I look back at my literary journey there was one moment which came just before my poetry book was completed. I believe it was a word from the Lord. On February 13, 2008 I was part of an online panel on Ella Curry's Black Author's Network Literary talk show. We were discussing "Black Love" on Black Love day, which is observed the day before Valentine's Day. I expressed my love for my wife as I always do and my thoughts on the energy required loving one woman compared to loving two. Impressed with how I handled myself Ms. Curry asked me to call in to speak with the guests who were on the following day.

On the air that evening was Essence and New York Times bestselling author, Mary B. Morrison. She is known for tremendous novels and having over seventeen titles. She gave the listeners an exciting discussion on women empowering their lives. She also gave advice on sexual pleasure which is in line with her genre of writing. The chat room was buzzing and the phone lines were packed. As I listened to the show and trying my best to keep up with the rapid pace of the chat room I decided to take Ms. Curry's advice and call in again.

By this time the show had moved into a conversation about why women were dating outside of their race. There were five women on and the conversation was in depth. When I called in I was the only one available to give the male perspective. Once the show ended I was thanked by Ms. Curry for the job I did and I was given a moment to give out my contact information. Well unknown to me the Lord was lining things up when I spoke on the show.

A few days later I received a call from Ella. I could hear in her voice that she was excited about what she was about to tell me.

"K. L., Ms. Morrison wants you in her new book, 'Who's Loving You?'"

Nothing she said was sinking into my brain like it should have. So she repeated it then asked, "Do you understand what I am saying to you? Mary B. Morrison wants you to write something that will be featured in her upcoming novel. She heard you on my show and she loved what you said about your wife and you overcoming the problems you had."

Now, it was registering. The author I had recently seen on the TV ONE network as one of the heavyweights in the African American writing business wants my story in her book. A woman who makes millions and travels the world because of her writing ability wants to do business with, essentially, an unknown as myself.

Over the next few days as I started to get my website together and make sure my professional look was in place it hit me. I am a Christian and Mary B. Morrison writes deep and strong sexual erotica. How can I write something to place in her book when her work is opposite my faith and beliefs? Here, in my upcoming book, I speak on how I changed my life from being a sexually charged erotic poet and short story artist to a romantic, socially conscious, and faith based author. So, I turned to the person I trust more than anyone in this world, my wife. I asked her what I should do since I didn't want to seem like a hypocrite because of an opportunity on the table.

"What did Ms. Morrison ask you to do?"

"She heard me on the radio show and she wants me to write about our story. She wants me to write about how you and I overcame all the cheating and problems we had."

After a few moments to think about it my wife said calmly, "Love, write our story just the way you told it. Don't change a word and if you're asked to change anything then excuse yourself from being a part of the book."

There it was. That was the direction I was going to take. I placed my trust in my wife and talents and sat and wrote the thirty-five hundred words asked for and sent the completed work to Ms. Morrison.

Two weeks passed and I hadn't heard anything. I started to feel as if I made a mistake. I started to think I blew my chance by writing about my faith and my relationship. But how do you compromise your faith when you know what is right for you? After thinking about it and praying on it I decided to call Ms. Morrison. I sat looking at the phone for a while then figured I had nothing to lose. I was so nervous I couldn't think. When the phone started to ring I was about to hang up like a teenage boy calling his school crush for the first time. Then Ms. Morrison picked up.

"Ms. Morrison, this is K. L. Belvin, you asked me to write something for your book." I continued, "We were on Ella Curry's radio show a few weeks back."

Before I could say another word she said, "The guy who loves his wife and said such beautiful words about her."

"Yes, that's me." Now, I'm smiling like a little child at the first sight of the tree on Christmas morning.

"Thank you, Ms. Morrison."

"Call me Mary."

"Thanks, Mary. I am calling because I wanted to ask what happen to my story." I was so nervous. "I followed all the directions you asked, but I haven't heard anything back from you."

"My people didn't get in touch with you?

"No."

"Oh, wait I will call them right now and have them send you the contract release form."

"Release form?"

"Of course. You have to sign a release for your story to be in my book."

"So, you're going to use it as it is?"

"Of course!" The excited tone in her voice was like music. "I loved what you wrote about you and your wife. This is what my readers need to see. You two have something real and I love to see relationships like that."

I was blown away. I got the stamp of approval from a world renowned author and here I was unsigned, unpublished and just starting out. Mary and I spoke for almost two hours. I can't even say it was a conversation it was me listening to her talk about the industry, her family, and her plans for the future. I think the idea of speaking to someone who was not in the limelight was a welcomed change from the norm for her.

Mary B. Morrison was so down to earth it made me start to understand the truth behind this blessing the Lord was granting me. People asked 'Why place your work in a book that has erotic stories?' My response is she reaches millions with her writing. When those readers come to her work to get whatever they are after, they will also get to see what the Lord is doing in my life. There is no way I could have set that up on my own, and now when someone walks into a books store they can pick up Mary B. Morrison's "Who's Loving You?" turn to page 246 and find my story.

By becoming a contributor to "Who's Loving You?" my writing career took a new turn. It felt different to me. I felt stronger about why I chose the literary industry. I know, technically, I am not the best writer who has penned a book. My passion and my feelings on certain subjects is what I am trying to express. My wife is the glue to my writing. Every piece I write goes to her to look over long before I send it out to be read. Our relationship is a product of a union which serves both of us. My weaknesses in writing are taken care of by the eyes the Lord has given my wife. I am a fantastic speaker and thinker, but I would be lost without someone who could pull all these thoughts I have and shape them into sense. It is from this union my first book was a success.

When you decide to write a poetry book you have to feel comfortable that money is not going to be dumped into a wheel barrel and left at your door. Poetry is a peculiar genre and when you decide to tell a story using it, you better have a reason people want to speak to you long before they hear your poems. Readers are fickle and their interest change like the tides of the oceans. Well this is where who I am compensates for this. When I tell my story and speak on what my wife and I have been through and then read a poem it helps my readers build a connection to me. I refuse to lose that connection with my readers.

I honestly believe readers want to feel a connection with the author through their words, but also with what they feel they know about the author. Now, I can sit here and try to sell you my style of writing as the best, but I will truthfully tell you it isn't when you line it up against the greats of the business. My style is basic and you will see the nuances many readers have come to love. I am not trying to entertain my readers. I simply want them to gain information, knowledge and clarity about my subjects. My wife pushes me to dig deeper into learning the art of writing and I have. As I grow and learn my ability to write will ascend also.

In creating Bravin Publishing my wife and I decided to build a platform which allowed authors to have a home to assist them in self-publishing their work. We wanted to present them with the idea that someday they would be in the same position I am in, right now, which is writing what I want and publishing my own books.

We decided to form this company which would open doors for others who felt compelled to share their craft, but were not appealing to the so-called giants in the literary world that wouldn't give them a second thought. Not bad for a young man who didn't read for fun.

Conclusion

Reconnecting with my faith has taught me to listen to my inner voice and find avenues to get my thoughts out. Being expressive was never a problem for me. It's one of the first things you learn when you decide to become a lady's man. What woman wouldn't want a man who's able to reach inside her and pull forth the type of feelings that can drive her to sexual bliss? However, things are so different now. What I'm trying to do now in my writing is drive home a message of comfort to my readers.

Considering the man that I am now and the changes I've made in my life mentally, emotionally, spiritually there's pain when I think of how I chose to live my life. There is also a sense of happiness. I'm happy I didn't end up with AIDS or an STD that I could have passed onto someone else, especially my wife. I'm happy I didn't create even more children than I already have. I use all of this as motivation to try to be a quality Teacher. To be an educator that students can respect. To be a father that can provide honest answers and give examples of my life to show them why they shouldn't make the same mistakes I did.

The meat of it is those changes were needed to fight with this addiction every day. It doesn't go away. Yes, I still live with a sexual addiction. I haven't stopped thinking about what it would be like to run out and go have sex with a lot of different women. I just don't allow those thoughts to control my actions. I still come across women who give subtle propositions although they know I'm married. Some of my past victims have even asked to be victimized again. They are okay with knowing that I am married and don't mind being used. It's not easy at all. I still view internet porn although I keep telling myself I don't need to let that demon in. I don't go to places, like strip clubs, where I know the focus is sex. I don't frequent bars and night clubs where an over indulgence of alcohol may dilute my judgment. I was willing to give all of those things up because the trade off was worth it. I feel comfortable with the choices I have made in my life now. So those small blessings and those small positives I cling to keep myself from being what I was.

If you are thinking about and doing something so often that it takes time away from every aspect of your life, if you're involved and have your thoughts connected to any particular thing so often that you find you're pulling away from things you should be involved in to be a part of what you shouldn't then you might have an addiction.

Whether it's drugs, gambling, alcohol, or sex, you should really consider getting help. You should consider making changes to the people in your circle. You should also consider being honest with yourself about who you really are. That's going to be the hardest step that you're ever going to have to take because that's where the real salvation, redemption, and healing are going to take place. It's also where the greatest struggle is going to take place.

When you get to the core, it is YOU versus YOU and you are a worthy opponent to yourself. I would say, before you face that battle arm yourself with faith that the Lord can pull you out of any situation. Have faith that you're not the only person dealing with this and the spiritual moves you're going to make will heal your wounds. Arm yourself with a boyfriend, girlfriend, brother, or sister—someone in your life who is going to dig in with you, lock arms with you and help you battle this demon you have inside of you.

Finally, arm yourself with forgiveness. Tell yourself that no matter what you've done you are now on the road to healing. Let your past go. That's what I do and I'm in such a better place now. Understand that I fight this everyday because I don't want to go backwards. Whatever point you are in your struggle keep in mind you're not alone. You'll share whatever you're doing with someone else because someone else needs your help as well as I pray they need mine too and will use this to help them.

I've realized that if we're going to change our community, we have to change our thinking and we have to change our living. It is my hope that I am an example of those two things and will continue to take a different route from where I started. I hope that you write down your own blueprint of everything that's going to make your dreams come true because if we don't, then we will not be able to overcome the death that comes from our sins. Then, what will we have? The same circle of negative energy repeating itself. We need to begin to change things right now. Starting with me as the writer, you as the reader, and all of us connected to each other under God.

www.ingramcontent.com/pod-product-compliance
Lightning Source LLC
LaVergne TN
LVHW041626070426
835507LV00008B/474